THE BALLAD OF
LES DARCY

THE BALLAD OF
LES DARCY

PETER FITZSIMONS

Books Alive is an Australian Government initiative
developed through the Australia Council for the Arts,
the Australian Government's arts funding and advisory body.

 HarperCollins*Publishers*

HarperCollins*Publishers*

First published in Australia in 2007
by HarperCollins*Publishers* Australia Pty Limited
ABN 36 009 913 517
www.harpercollins.com.au

HarperCollins*Publishers*
25 Ryde Road, Pymble, Sydney, NSW 2073, Australia
31 View Road, Glenfield, Auckland 10, New Zealand
77–85 Fulham Palace Road, London W6 8JB, United Kingdom
2 Bloor Street East, 20th floor, Toronto, Ontario M4W 1A8, Canada
10 East 53rd Street, New York NY 10022, USA

National Library of Australia Cataloguing-in-Publication data:

FitzSimons, Peter.
    The ballad of Les Darcy.
    ISBN 13: 978 0 7322 8636 1 (pbk.).
    1. Darcy, Les, 1895–1917. 2. Boxers (Sports) – Australia –
    Biography. 3. Boxing – Australia. I. Title.
796.830994

Cover design by Matt Stanton
Cover images: New York – Getty, image 10150339; WWI troops – Australian War
Memorial, image H11588; Winnie O'Sullivan – Kevin Hannan Collection,
reprographer Dean McNicoll, National Museum of Australia, image nma.img-
ci20061709-005; feather – Shutterstock, image 1976548.
Typeset in 11/13.5 Bembo by Kirby Jones
Printed and bound in Australia by McPherson's Printing Group
on 70gsm Ensocreamy

5 4 3 2 1   07 08 09 10

To Les Darcy himself;

and to the two men who, over forty years,

each did more than any others to document his story,

D'Arcy Niland and Bob Power

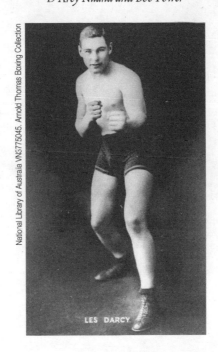

INTRODUCTION

Late in 2005, I received a phone call from HarperCollins publishing director Shona Martyn saying that I had been selected to be the 2007 author for the Books Alive program. This, she explained, would involve me writing a manuscript of some forty to fifty thousand words on any subject of my choice, with two or three hundred thousand copies being distributed around the country in the winter of that year.

Oh.

Thank you.

And put me down as a 'Yes, please!'

In response to the wonderful opportunity, I considered many options, many possible themes to warm to, stories to tell, several of which I persisted with for hours, days and even *weeks* at a time, until I lost interest and the whole thing ... kinda ... sorta ... petered ... out.

Yeah.

In the end, however, it was a chance conversation with my friend Matthew Reilly, who was the Books Alive author of 2005, followed by another conversation shortly afterwards with the Chair of Books Alive, Sandra Yates, which steered me in the right direction.

'Do the stuff you do best,' Matthew said. 'Write the kind of story you most love.'

Cue Sandra: 'You've got to understand,' she said, 'what an enormous readership this is. You have to write the story that you most wish other Australians knew about.'

Bingo! For, using those two bits of advice, the choice of my subject became a lot easier.

The thing I do best — or at least the thing I feel most passionate about — is writing stories from Australia's past. And of those that I had come across, there were two stories that particularly worked my spirit, stories which I thought were finer than any others I'd heard any time, any place — stories I wished were more widely known to my fellow Australians. They are the story of the shipwreck of the *Batavia* off the west coast of Australia in 1629, and the saga of the great Australian boxer Les Darcy, which reached its climax as Australia blooded itself as a nation in World War I.

Back in the mid–1980s, my rugby coach was the Australian author Peter Fenton, and of the many yarns he used to relate, the story of Les Darcy was foremost. Peter himself went on to publish a book on Les in 1994, *Les Darcy: The Legend of the Fighting Man*, which I enjoyed, as I did the fascinating book on Darcy written by Ruth Park and Rafe Champion called *Home Before Dark*, which followed shortly afterwards.

I had intended to write a story of just 2,000 words on Darcy for a book on great Australian sporting champions called *Everyone and Phar Lap*, but the saga had refused to be so contained and it had blown out considerably. Still, the thing that had gnawed at me was that the ballad of Les Darcy remained to the Australian public not a hundredth as well known as the ones so often told of Phar Lap and Don Bradman, even though in the first half of last century Don Bradman – Phar Lap – Les Darcy had been almost the Holy Trinity of Australian sport stories. In 1947 the readers of the Australian magazine *Sports Novels* voted Les Darcy the greatest sportsman of all time — and this while Bradman was still batting! And as recently as the fifty-year anniversary of Les's death, in 1967, well-attended commemorative services were held and a memorial marking his birthplace in Maitland was unveiled by the former Governor-General Sir William McKell.

Just why the Darcy story has faded in the popular imagination I know not, but I am certain that if given a chance to breathe in the twenty-first century it will live again, as it deserves to.

In terms of how to tell it, I kept coming back to a few lines that leaped out at me in the course of my research, written by one T.J. Moran in the *Newcastle Morning Herald and Miners Advocate* on 20 May 1967:

> It is difficult to write anything new about a champion
> who has been the subject of so many tens of thousands
> of words in numerous newspapers and magazine articles
> and in at least three books ...

Some day, someone will collect the threads of the Darcy story and write about the times in which he lived, will tell of the tragedy and drama of a young life that became a legend and a symbol (for and against) for all those people caught up in the turbulence of World War I, the conscription issue, the influence of the Irish Easter Rebellion of 1916, the Dr Mannix Statements, the strong emotions that rocked Australia and that brushed on to a young man whose real conflict was that of love of family versus love of country . . .

I do not, make no mistake, claim to be that person — and I encourage readers who get absorbed by the story to read Peter Fenton's *Les Darcy* and Ruth Park and Rafe Champion's *Home Before Dark* to fill out their knowledge of the Darcy tale. But again and again, in framing the story that is well known to the aficionados, I kept coming to the conclusion that you can't appreciate Les's story unless you really do have a basic understanding of the times in which he lived — of what the conscription debate was about, what Dr Mannix said, why the Easter Rebellion in Ireland had such an impact in Australia — and the consequent dilemmas the boxer faced because of all this.

In terms of unearthing new material and expanding the narrative from my original portrait, I put considerable effort into researching the fate of those of Les's friends and contemporaries who made a different choice from him when it came to the Great War. Of those friends, I became fascinated with Eric Newton in particular — and in all the research I have done for all my books, no moment has ever hit me harder than when I put the pieces together and worked out what had happened to Eric.

All those who attempt to tell the story of Darcy are hampered by the problem of working out what is myth and what is fact, as you sift through successive layers of storytelling through every generation. To get around that, where possible I have gone to original documents and reports. I've also leaned most heavily on those publications with a track record of truth. In my view two authors stand out in this regard. The first is Ruth Park's husband, the great Australian writer D'Arcy Niland, who was named after Darcy and who spent many decades researching his story, often in the company of Ruth Park. After his death, she and her son-in-law Rafe Champion used that material to write the aforementioned *Home Before Dark* — and I thank Rafe for his encouragement and advice throughout this project.

The second is a former postmaster from Newcastle by the name of Bob Power. In 1976 he wrote and self-published *Fighters of the North*, a finely researched account of boxers in the Hunter Valley around the turn of last century, and he followed this up in 1994 with an absolute gem of a book, *The Les Darcy American Venture*, which he also self-published. Mr Power's strength is that he has not only spent years ferreting out minute detail, but has also talked to many of the surviving protagonists, like Les Fletcher, Father Joe Coady, Tim O'Sullivan and even the chief bosun on the *Hattie Luckenbach*, a ship that was most significant in his story. For someone like me trying to revive a story nigh on a hundred years old, with no contemporary survivors anywhere, it was a wonderful bonus to find that, though ninety-seven years old, Mr Power was still hale and hearty, and was happy to help me in this quest to try and get to the essence of my subject. I warmly thank him for his generosity of spirit, and dips my lid to him as an author and truly great researcher. I will long treasure the memory of sitting with him for many hours in his kitchen and in his back-yard garage, surrounded by photos of Les Darcy, going through detail after detail, and coming away with riches.

Let me also take the opportunity to thank the many others who provided their personal and professional expertise. I cite particularly Glenda Lynch, who worked tirelessly at the Australian War Memorial; Terri McCormack, who scoured many old newspaper files for me from libraries across the country; the staff and especially Robert Woodley of the Mitchell Library, Sydney; Tony Edmunds of the *Maitland Mercury*; Aaron Pegram of the National Museum of Australia, Canberra; Bronwyn Ryan of the Australian National Library; Jennifer and Walter Buffier and their family, who now live in the Darcy house of Lesleigh in East Maitland and who were so wonderfully welcoming to me; Ann Mitchell of the *Newcastle Herald* archives; Robert Reid, the Chairman of the Les Darcy Committee; Peter Woodley of East Maitland Library; William Edwards of the National Archives of Australia; Gionni DiGravio of Newcastle University Library; local Maitland historian Cameron Archer; Julie Cox of the Catholic Diocese of Maitland-Newcastle; and Winnie

O'Sullivan's surviving son, Father Kevin Hannan, who was very helpful with reminiscences of his mother.

This is my eighteenth book, and by this time I have been blessed with a very good team of people helping me to put it together. My warm thanks go to my principal researcher, Sonja Goernitz, who was as indefatigable as ever in scouring the great institutions of our land for whatever treasures or traces of Darcy they might have, and extremely generous in sharing her writing instincts with me. My deep gratitude also to my treasured colleague at the *Sydney Morning Herald*, Harriet Veitch, who put many weekend and evening hours into the project, sorting out my mangled sentences and the like. Kevin Brumpton has worked with me for the last ten years retrieving verifiable information from the internet, and I will remain in his debt for his great work on this book, too.

I record my appreciation and professional respect to everyone I worked with at HarperCollins, most particularly Shona Martyn, Alison Urquhart, Matt Stanton, Mary Rennie, Graeme Jones and David Morgan.

Finally, my deepest affection to my wife, Lisa Wilkinson. As a professional editor, she improves everything I write and this book was no exception. As my wife, and mother of our children, she carries an extra burden over many months when my body is strapped behind the study desk, and my mind is perpetually elsewhere — in this case with Les and his family — instead of with her and our family.

What follows is my take on the Les Darcy story using a technique I have warmed to in recent books, which has been to try and make a non-fiction book at least *feel* like a novel, albeit resting on the thousand points of light which are established and endnoted fact. I write this at a time when there is frequently discussion in the public domain about just what the best way to get young Australians interested in our history is. I don't have any definitive answer, but allow me to say that from my own point of view the only way I can get interested in writing it — at which point I love it — is to try and get the subject to *breathe*, to live, to ride again!

To do so, occasionally, sparingly, I have used poetic licence, as in when I surmise at one point how wrenching it must have been for Les to take his leave of the love of his life, without having the documentary proof of this. Nor do I have proof of what it must have been like to be up against Darcy in the ring. It is my view that at such moments of shared human response it is worth whipping out my licence to preserve the flow and feel of the story, even if that means I am prevented from indulging in three or four paragraphs of earnest discussion as to just what his feelings might have been at the time.

This does not pretend to be *the* comprehensive biography, because that is simply not possible in only 50,000 words. The Darcy demons will note that I have effectively skimmed over such things as the controversies surrounding the Jeff Smith fights, the second Fritz Holland fight, Les's exact commercial relationship with 'Sully', the precise whys and wherefores of H.D. McIntosh's involvement in what happened in America and so forth. They are all worthy subjects but too weighty for this slim volume.

What I most want is for readers to get into the wonder of the Les Darcy story and the extraordinary times in which he lived.

I hope you enjoy the reading . . . as I enjoyed the writing.

PETER FITZSIMONS
SYDNEY
APRIL 2007

1

Way Back When

Yes, a gallant lad, simple and honest, with an abiding courage. His successful, if short, career should be an object lesson to all Australian boys. When they remember how Les Darcy rose from the ruck to the heights, they too can emulate the spirit that was left, in Tennyson's words, 'footprints in the sands of time'.

DAVE SMITH, FORMER DARCY TRAINER AND OPPONENT[1]

He had three arms, possibly four. He hit you with one jawbreaker, had another waiting four inches behind it, and a third on the way.

DAVE DEPENA, AN AMERICAN WHO WAS ONE OF THE FIRST OF DARCY'S OPPONENTS TO GAIN MORE OF AN ACQUAINTANCE WITH THE CANVAS THAN HE WAS EXPECTING

She is an old woman, walking down the aisle of St Francis' Church in Paddington, on the bright, clear morning of 24 May 1967, in the company of a handsome priest. If recognition does not come to everyone in the packed church immediately, it certainly seeps through now, as she moves further into the dappled light provided by the towering stained-glass windows, and her still fine features become more apparent. Yes, indeed, that is *her*.

Mrs Winifred Hannan of Bondi, just nearing seventy years old, has the bearing of one who — if not necessarily to the manor born — could at least take her place in any manor in the land and look like she belongs there. Winifred is a lady, in the best sense of the word, a woman of natural class and regal bearing, yet all of it without the tiniest sniff of snootiness.

And as she makes her way to her seat, down the front on the left, next to the former Governor-General Sir William McKell, those few who are not yet aware that she is here are now nudged and whisperingly told by others.

'Winnie ...' 'Winifred O'Sullivan.' 'That's her ...' 'She was Les's girl ...' 'Darcy's sweetheart ...' 'Fifty years ago to the day ...' 'She was with him when he ...' 'They were going to be married in ...'

Can Winnie hear the polite stirring behind? Perhaps. Perhaps not.

For the moment she simply sits there, gazing forward, looking at the massive crucifix above the altar, and doing what she often does, which is to open and close the tiny gold locket she has kept, wherein lies a lock of Les's hair and her favourite photo of him, beaming. She has done it so many times over the last fifty years that her thumb print is worn into its lid, and yet none of her family knows of the locket's existence.

Is she, too, thinking of what might have happened in this very church all those years ago if things had turned out differently?

The locket belonging to Winnie O'Sullivan, which she lovingly kept secret all her life.

Ah, but already we're ahead of ourselves. For the story of Les Darcy, Winifred O'Sullivan, and what happened between them we need go back a fair ways, back to old Ireland ...

Too many people. Not enough food.

It got so bad that just about the entire class of common labourers known as *cottiers* were wiped out, with estimates of 750,000 dead. The devastating blight that hit the Irish potato crop in the latter part of the 1840s turned what should have been food into a soggy, black, poisonous mess, and a terrible starvation took hold of the land, in a death grip that simply would not let go, with the cities particularly hard hit. In early 1849, a Dublin barrister recorded that while doing his rounds he frequently came across children who were 'almost naked, hair standing on end, eyes sunken, lips pallid, protruding bones of little joints visible.'[2] In a village just outside the capital a woman had been driven mad with hunger and eaten parts of her own dead children, while other people — still sane — managed just to stay alive by killing and eating the very dogs which had been feeding off dead bodies.[3] Normally honest citizens were so desperate to get away they committed crimes in the hope they would be arrested and transported to Australia. 'Even if I had chains on my legs, I would still have something to eat . . .' said one Irish teenager after his arrest.[4]

Many of the survivors of the first famine emigrated in the more regular fashion, and every successive famine thereafter prompted another outgoing tide. In just two decades at least three million people of the pre-famine population of eight million left the Emerald Isle. They didn't quite know what they were heading to, but they sure knew what they were leaving behind: a slow, starving death. What they took with them was a great love of Ireland and enormous bitterness at the land's British rulers who — through the worst of the famines — had simply sat on their hands and done *nothing* while people died. The famine, in the view of Charles Trevelyan, the assistant secretary of the British Treasury, was simply a 'mechanism for reducing surplus population'. And as to what caused it, he was in no doubt. 'The judgement of God sent the calamity to teach the Irish a lesson,' he wrote in 1848, 'and that calamity must not be too much mitigated . . . The real evil with which we have to contend is not the physical evil of the Famine, but the moral evil of the selfish, perverse and turbulent character of the people.'[5]

Under British control, thus Ireland had been throughout the famine a net exporter of thousands upon thousands of tons of corn, even while its own people died for want of such a precious staple. When violent protests broke out about the export of the corn, an activity over which Trevelyan presided, he sent in 2,000 armed British troops to quell them. Many of the Irish at home and abroad would never forgive this and other British outrages, and the momentum of a violent separatist movement, committed to Ireland establishing Home Rule, free from the British, began to gather weight . . .

A part of that tide was the O'Rourke clan — a family boasting four young adult brothers and a sister — and while the Hunter Valley, north of Sydney Town was, to be sure, a long, long way from Tipperary, when they arrived there in the mid-1850s they had little doubt that the journey had been worth it. For, in the Hunter Valley, as they were delighted to find, the rivers ran long and wide, the grass grew lush and green, the people were basically cheery, and the land was at peace. Why, on a good day it could even look the way the Emerald Isle used to be. It was the kind of place to make a life, and the O'Rourkes did exactly that, quickly making an impression.

Whatever else, they were physically strong people and one story that entered local legend was how a shopkeeper bet family matriarch Mrs O'Rourke a bag of flour weighing 200 pounds that she couldn't carry it a distance of 50 yards. Mrs O'Rourke accepted the bet and not only carried it the 50 yards, but, for good measure, kept right on going all the way home, over a mile away![6]

As to her children, the eldest, Michael O'Rourke, was the wild one. When, on occasion, the problems of the old world surfaced again in Australia, and the Catholic 'Greens' would delight in setting upon a parade of the Protestant Irish 'Orangemen' — Michael would habitually cut a swathe through those British loyalists, his fists flying all the way.[7]

Terence O'Rourke, the second child, though even more powerfully built than his older brother, was t' gentler one n'all, known to be so fond of dancing an Irish jig that he would carry a sheet of a stringybark with him to work and when the mood took hold he would lie it rough-side down so he could dance to his heart's content on the shiny side — and he is the one who concerns us now.[8]

See, the O'Rourkes were breeders, and after Terence married into the Hough clan, his wife soon enough produced five sons and five daughters, of whom the youngest one was Margaret. A lovely girl, Margaret, devout and hard-working . . . but headstrong! When she took it into her head that she wanted to do something, there was simply no stopping her, and so it was with marrying Ned Darcy, whom she spied one day doing some work out on the Seaham road. She liked the cut of his jib, his gentle manner, his politeness, and she just didn't *care* about the other things . . .

Ah, t'other things . . .

Like the O'Rourkes, the Darcys were classic Irish-Australian stock: proud, plentiful and Catholic to their very core, so there was no problem on that account. But *Ned* Darcy, for their young Margaret? Why, Ned was a poor widower, eleven years older than her, a man who already had a couple of adolescent children. And could he drink! Terence O'Rourke, for one, was not happy, and as a matter of fact, because Margaret was still under twenty-one years of age, he had the right, if he so chose, to deny her permission to wed. In the end, however, the will of his daughter was stronger than his own, and she persuaded him to sign the relevant document. Still, he had his misgivings. What kind of life awaited the far more genteel Margaret after she married a rough man like that?

Whatever else, it was a full one. After marrying on 4 July 1893, at St Bede's Church in Morpeth, just outside of Maitland, the couple were to have twelve babies, of whom ten survived their infancy, ensuring a highly cramped existence in the rough three-bedroom shack that would soon serve as Ned and Margaret Darcy's home on an even rougher, rented, nearby dairy farm called Pitnacree. Of those babies, Les was the second-born, arriving in late October 1895.

Ned, who worked as something of an itinerant labourer, was never quite as fruitful as his loins when it came to providing *for* his family, but still did the best he could, sort of. Essentially, he drifted along from job to job as they came up, without ever seeming to row too hard between times. Though basically a good and decent man, Ned really could be a demon on the drink, and in the bad times he never seemed to be off it.

Again, it became the stuff of local lore that on one occasion when Margaret was in real trouble during a difficult labour, Ned had run across the paddocks to get some brandy from a neighbour to settle her down but, well, one thing led to another and ... and he ended up drinking it all himself before he got back to her.[9]

Despite Ned's failings, though, family life at Pitnacree was not without its good things and most of them emanated from mother Margaret. While it is a moot point whether she had quite the physical strength of her grandmother, who had so famously carried the bag of flour all the way home, she certainly wasn't far off it — but it was her moral strength that so inspired everyone. Margaret was a woman whose every effort, every day, was devoted to seeing her family grow and prosper. Rising at dawn, she was the sun around which the rest of the family revolved, providing light, warmth and direction.

Whatever the Darcys' material circumstances at any given time — from so poor they didn't have two beans to rub together, all the way up to just struggling by — she ensured that her offspring were as well turned out as they could possibly be, that their manners were impeccable, that her children attended Mass, that they were honest, hard-working and forthright, and never swore or blasphemed. And of Margaret's children none was closer to their mother than Les, whom she affectionately called 'Bub'.

With Ned Darcy being the way he was, and Les's older brother Cecil being crippled with a severely turned-in foot, it is not surprising that young Les grew towards manhood with a strong feeling in his breast that it was his responsibility to ease the terrible burden on his mother, his *duty* to try and lift his family out of poverty.

Most of his father's meagre wages wound up in the hands of the local hoteliers, meaning that the family's real survival money came from the Pitnacree cows. It thus fell to young Les, before school and after it, to not only do such regular household chores as chop the wood and haul the coal, but also to move the cows and milk them. If this meant that Les generally grew up busier than a blowfly in March, it also had one other important spin-off. For all the farm work and physical activity helped make an already naturally strong body even stronger. Indeed, what had bubbled up from the combined Darcy–O'Rourke gene pool in Les's case was singularly impressive.

While the Darcys were famous for their athleticism, the O'Rourkes were equally renowned for their strength and agility, and Les always had those three physical qualities in full measure. He wasn't tall — fully grown he was only about five foot, seven inches. But he was perfectly formed in a compact, thickset kind of way, and the obvious bull strength of his neck was testament to how well his head was attached to his shoulders, just as his modest manner bespoke one whose feet were always firmly on the ground. Les was ever and always friendly to a fault, as polite a person as you'd meet in six days' march, just as his mother had taught him to be. And fun to be around — laughing, joking, all the time, he had charisma enough to kill a brown dog. This effervescent sunny outlook was coupled with a fierce belief in Catholicism. Mass was *never* missed. Yet there still remained plenty of room in the boy's soul for a passion that you mightn't expect to find in one so generously and religiously disposed.

Boxing . . .

Whatever his natural gentleness and even gentility, Les loved nothing better than testing his wits and mitts against others. From his first rough-and-tumbles with his brothers around the dairy to fighting in the schoolyard, he adored boxing above all else bar his mother, who, for her part, was forever worrying that her beloved 'Bub' would be hurt while engaged in his pugilism.

Mind though, in this concern and her distaste for the sport, Margaret Darcy was very much in the minority. For it wasn't just young Les who loved boxing, not by a long shot. All over the Hunter where Les was growing up boxing was the rage! In the schoolyards, on the streets, behind the pubs, squaring off in makeshift 'rings', lads and full-grown men were 'putting their dukes up'!

Right up until the late 1890s, bare-knuckle fighting had been the rule — with each opponent going at it, until one fell, a bloodied mess — before bit by bit giving way to these gloved contests.

See, for starters the folks who populated the world of Les Darcy, drawn from the farms, vineyards, mines, timber camps and lumber mills that abounded all around the area, were above all a *physical* people. And there was, of course, no more physical sport than boxing, where two blokes, four fists and lots of courage were pretty much all you needed to get started. Maybe the origin of the great Australian term 'battlers' was in that it described the usual financial plight of the workers at this time; or perhaps it was in that it was their favourite pastime. Either way, the point was that if you got the battling in the ring right, you no longer had to battle financially. Why, look at the Australian legend, 'Young Griffo', the hero to beat them all, who had started life as Albert Griffiths, a humble Sydney dock worker who, through the force of his fists, had made a fortune, gone all the way to America and finished up fighting for the featherweight championship of the world!

Though Les Darcy's early promise at boxing was noted by his schoolmates, it wasn't really until — in order to help to support his family — he left his school attached to St Joseph's convent at the age of twelve and took up a round as a milk-carter that the rest of his tight world started to take some notice. At that time in the 12,000 strong town of Maitland, it was something of a tradition that the milk-cart boys and the stable hands from around the area would meet on Sunday mornings behind Cush's stable, out on Oakhampton Road. There, within a rough ring of milk carts, they would have a series of informal boxing matches — often refereed by old Jack Cush himself, smoking his pipe. The best of them, if their imaginations were fired wild, could even dream that one day, if they proved themselves good enough, one day, they could be in a *real* boxing match down at Sydney's Rushcutters Bay, where this amazing stadium had just opened up!

They called it the 'Sydney Stadium', a slightly grandiose name given that it consisted of nothing more than an elevated open-air boxing ring, sitting on a floor of bare hammered earth, on a spot that used to be known as Billygoat Swamp,[10] surrounded by row after row of tiered seating. Sure, it was as rough as guts, but no other stadium south of the equator could claim to hold more.

The Stadium's famous inauguration into the real big time — after a smaller bout five months earlier — came on Boxing Day 1908, with nothing less than a bout to determine who was the heavyweight champion of the world! Les and his friends up in Maitland were agog with the excitement of it all, just as were the sporting communities of Australia, America and Canada, not to mention other countries where boxing held sway, such as Britain, France and much of the rest of Europe.

For the set-up to this particular bout was unprecedented. Not only was it the first heavyweight championship in Australia, but the particularities of the two opponents attracted enormous interest ...

In one corner, Tommy Burns, a rough, tough Canadian from Ontario, who had been world champion since 1906. In the other, black Jack Johnson, the son of two slaves, who hailed from the badlands of Galveston, Texas, where he had begun his career by brutally fighting other black men for the amusement of the rich white local folk — in bare-knuckle fights with no rules, known as 'battle royals', where the winner was the last man left standing.

Now, the major barrier to Johnson being world champion was the common view that a black man should *not* fight a white man in proper championship bouts — for fear that if the black man won, the whole Negro race might get 'uppity'. In the absence of white men to beat, Johnson had worked his way through the great black American fighters of the day, including Sam McVey, Joe Jeanette and the 'Boston Tar Baby' Sam Langford. It had been frustrating for Johnson to see Tommy Burns crowned as world champion when Burns hadn't yet had the pleasure of meeting him in the ring, but he soon enough hit on a plan to smoke the 'world champion' out from deep cover so he could be killed in the open. For months, Johnson followed Burns around the world, to New York, London and Paris, sitting in the front row during his fights and calling out that the Canadian wasn't the *true* world champion until he had beaten him, Johnson.

It so happened that in the last gasp of 1908, Burns was fighting in New Zealand, when the deal came together ...

The Australian businessman who owned the Sydney Stadium, a hard-nosed harrier by the name of H.D. McIntosh, offered Burns the largest amount of prize money ever offered to a boxer — £7,500 — if he would fight Johnson in Sydney on Boxing Day, 1908.

An interesting man, McIntosh, and it was not just because of his initials 'H.D.' that he was known as 'Huge Deal'. Fact was, this ruthless social climber, who was about three or four parts charm to one part menace, who knew *everybody* and was even rumoured to have the NSW Premier, William Holman, in his pocket, as well as being very close to the Federal Attorney-General, Billy Hughes, really did bring off Huge Deals, and it was typical of him to think that he could bring off something as big as a heavyweight championship of the world in Sydney. Certainly, if anyone could do it, Huge Deal could. And for that kind of money Burns had no hesitation in accepting; even though Johnson was to receive only £1,500, the American also agreed. A sign of the trust that both boxers had in McIntosh was that they agreed that the promoter himself could be the referee.

So it was on, and up Maitland way Les and his mates followed the lead-up closely, just as people all over Australia did — the vast majority hoping that the black man would be trounced. And look there, what it says in the paper! Three weeks before the bout was due, shortly after he arrived in Australia, Burns announced: 'I'll beat the nigger or my name isn't Tommy Burns.'[11] Now the fact that his birth name *wasn't*

Tommy Burns, but Noah Brusso, might have given a fair indication to the final result, but after just three rounds of the fight the likelihood is that not even the Canadian knew if he was Tommy or Noah — or Arthur or Martha!

See, from the opening bell, Jack Johnson had been like a lion toying with a sick rabbit in the person of Tommy Burns, a rabbit that Johnson was in no mood to kill quickly and put out of its misery. After the first flurry of blows Johnson was heard to shout: 'Here I am, Tommy. Who told you I was yellow?'

He wasn't yellow, he was *black*, and he was angry. A 'nigger' was he? That what you said, Tommy? You were going to beat the nigger?

Right cross. Sickening uppercut. Blow to the ribs.

Going to show the 'nigger' who was *'massah'*, was he? Well, let's see it!

Left hook. Straight right.

The 20,000 strong crowd at the Sydney Stadium roared as Johnson kept throwing his punches, and there were more watching than just the people with seats. On the high ground of the neighbouring suburb of Paddington, on the veranda of the top floor of their Lord Dudley Hotel, most of the large and sprawling O'Sullivan family was watching the bout eagerly, their view to the Stadium uninterrupted.

The boxing, *per se*, did not interest the two young sisters of the clan, Winnie and Eileen — no females raised to be proper young ladies would ever show too much interest in such an activity — but the spectacle of it all certainly did, and the fact that it so fascinated the male members of their family.

For Winnie's part she couldn't quite understand why two men hitting each other should arouse such excitement, but evidently her older brother, Maurice, for one, was totally absorbed and constantly jumped up and down with excitement as he watched the two distant figures clash again and again, before the white figure typically fell back, reeling. Despite the distance, the difference in the boxers' skin colour made it easy for the watchers on the cast-iron balcony to work out Johnson was having far and away the best of it, if not quite comprehending the fine detail.

Down ringside, a bloke by the name of 'Gentleman' Dave Smith, a young boxer from a mining town just outside of Dunedin, New Zealand, who a few months before had won the NSW amateur light heavyweight title, saw the whole thing close up, with eyes expert enough to appreciate just how truly skilled, and savage, Johnson was — despite some spectators willing Burns on to kill him!

Round after round, Johnson would strike through Burns's feeble defences, hit him hard enough to daze but not fell him, and then, with a big gold-toothed grin, *invite* Burns to take his best shot! And like a desperately sick rabbit, Burns would try a couple of exhausted swipes with his paws, whereupon Johnson would whack him *again,* still careful not to fell him. A few times when it seemed that Burns would drop, Johnson was even seen to hold him up, to get him to the end of the round so that he could take a fresh beating next round.

Oh, Mistuh Tommy, you shouldn't oughta have been so rude about me.

By the fourteenth round, however, Johnson was tired of the pretence and roared in to finish it, raining blow after blow all over Burns. It was at this point that the cameras rolling to show the bout in cinemas around the world were turned off so that this terrible humiliation of the white race would *not* be recorded for posterity. After all, what decent folk wanted to see the preening, prancing black man continue to humiliate the bleeding, stumbling white man? Cut! Cut! CUT!

So savage was Johnson's last barrage that even the most bloodthirsty screamed for the massacre to cease and, rather than merely the referee, it was in fact the police who moved in to stop it, swarming into the ring to end what had stopped being a boxing match and was now no more than a flagrant 'assault and battery'.

Jack Johnson was crowned the first black heavyweight champion of the world, and the resultant publicity made boxing more popular in Australia than ever.

Seven thousand, five hundred pounds for losing!

For a nation where the average working man's weekly wage was just £3, the figure was breathtaking, and encouraged more than ever young men with boxing talent to dream that one day they too might be able to win such an amount.

Up behind Cush's stable every Sunday morning, of course, the most common prize was a bloody nose and a black eye, but Les Darcy received fewer than most, such was his growing skill. Two things particularly distinguished Les in his early fights at this venue. Firstly, far from having a 'glass jaw', as the expression went, Les seemed to have one made of granite. It mattered naught whether he took a straight right cross on the chin or a full-blooded left hook; it never rattled him! And, perhaps even more importantly, whatever his natural talents, Les was a learner. Other young aspiring boxers had a set style of whaling away and, fancying they already knew most of what there was to know about the caper — after all, you were unlikely to get into a ring at all unless you were already a confident character — didn't change their style from one week to the next. But not young Darcy. From the beginning, Les was a listener who seemed keen to soak up as much knowledge as he could, and developed his style from week to week.

One who noticed Les's talent early on, and liked very much of what he saw, was his local parish priest, Father Joe Coady, a classic red-headed cleric — all sharp angles in appearance and soft roundness inside — who had given the young boy instruction on being confirmed into Roman Catholicism and met him every morning at Mass thereafter. Not just Sundays — *every* morning. Now, while Father Joe loved the Lord, he possibly loved sport almost as much, and though his love of horse racing was strong enough that he delighted in using a retired racehorse as his means of transportation around the township, he also knew a little about boxing. And so now, as well as providing religious guidance, Father Joe frequently mixed it with a little boxing instruction in the afternoons, and the foundation of what would become an extraordinarily strong friendship between the two was laid. Father Coady had himself hailed from a large, bright and bustling family of thirteen children from nearby Scone — of whom no fewer than five of his sisters were nuns — and somehow around the Darcys he felt very much at home.

The real boxing breakthrough? That came when Les was about fifteen years old and doing some itinerant work on the construction of new railway cuttings between Newcastle and Maitland, near the locality of Thornton. While, for the most part, it was the job of grown men to blast the stone, break it with sledgehammers and then shift it, it was for the likes of Les to take their horses and drays and load them up with stone before — *giddy up* — carrying the stone away to unload it at another spot further down the line. This, for all concerned, was brutal, backbreaking work beneath the hot sun, with the dust, the noise, the sheer throbbing, gut-busting nature of it making men roll their eyes in exhaustion — so what better way to relax at the end of the day, and even occasionally at lunch time, than to hit each other?

This was frequently done in rough boxing matches — both bare-fisted and with gloves — and, of course, it didn't take long before the other men noticed how well young Darcy handled himself.

How well?

I say so well I reckon he could beat Balser!

Oh yeah? Well *I* say he couldn't and I have five shillings to my name to back it up!

Yer on!

And so it was done.

George 'Guvnor' Balser was a 21-year-old former jockey who'd turned his hand to boxing, and was also now working on the site. And he was no joke, this cove. Looking like he had been carved out of the very rock that they had all been cutting through, Guvnor was a hard man, and with all his vast experience, his supporters felt it was crazy to even suggest that the 15-year-old Darcy could hold his own against him, but strangely the young'un lacked no backers who swore he could take the older man down!

In the lead-up to the bout, the workers quickly split into two camps, of Darcy supporters and Balser loyalists, with loads of bets made accordingly and prize money set up for the boxers themselves.

Come the afternoon of the designated Sunday in December of 1910, a line of wire was strung up around some saplings, the workers gathered and all was ready. *Ding-ding,* went the spanner on a tucker-box. *ROAR* went the workers gathered round as the two boxers, man and boy, moved towards each other. The referee for the occasion was one of the powder-monkeys, an expert in working with high explosives, which was as well, under the circumstances ...

Geez, you shoulda been there! Right from the first it was clear that Darcy was more than happy to trade blows with this fully grown man. It wasn't just Les's obvious gameness that impressed, and nor was it that he also clearly knew how to both give and take a punch. No, it was the sheer enjoyment he displayed while moving around the makeshift ring as the workers screamed their blood-lusty support.

The kid was — get this — *smiling*, all the way through the bout. It wasn't an arrogant smile of the *nyah-nyah*-can't-hurt-me variety, nor even was it a maddeningly superior I'm-better-than-you-and-I-know-it grin. Rather, as was apparent to all those watching, Les Darcy simply *loved* to box, and the pleasure it gave him would brook no hiding ... whether he was giving or taking one. For round after round the two workers went at it, a donnybrook for the ages, as their two groups of backers roared their encouragement in the way only men who have as much as a week's wages riding on the outcome can. So evenly matched were they that after ten rounds of two minutes' duration each, the referee said they were too equal to pick a winner. It was decided that they should go at it for one more round. Again the two men disappeared into a whistling whirl of punches, flying sweat, and grunts and groans, as the fighters threw and took many hard blows.

At last, though, it was over. And the winner is ... in the gum tree cornerrrrrr ... Les Darcyyyyyy!

The young man was away. His prize money for the win came to the princely sum of fifteen shillings, something like three weeks' wages for him — and before taking it home he was sure to convert it into one penny pieces so he could laughingly throw it all over his mother's bed. She, in turn, was able to use it to buy the family a much-needed second-hand stove. The pride in young Les as the stove was installed was overflowing, but mixed with pride was a resolution — to redouble his efforts in the boxing ring to bring even larger rewards home to his family in the future.[12]

That notwithstanding, Margaret Darcy still made it clear to her beloved son that she wished he wouldn't box, as she was fearful for his safety. And yet she equally knew that she was all but powerless to curtail the major passion of Les's life, particularly when he could see how much the money he provided was needed.

Although Father Joe Coady was not at the fight against Balser, Les's victory confirmed the priest's view that Les might very well have a promising future in this sport, and it was at his suggestion that Les met up with a rough-and-tumble knockabout Maitland bloke with the unlikely name of Michaelangelo Hawkins — better known as Mick Hawkins — who was about ten years older than Les.

Mick was a special case, the kind of rough-nut-with-a-heart-of-gold that every country town has and more or less values without necessarily knowing quite what his full story is. With a squashed nose and bad limp as evidence, Mick claimed to be a former footballer, while others whispered on the quiet that the limp, at least, was from childhood polio, and the rest was just Mick blarney, y'know? Either way it didn't matter. The main thing was that Mick — a gardener-cum-labourer-cum-broke-and-unemployed — had a good heart, a keen eye for sporting talent, and among other things dabbled in training young footballers and boxers. Father Coady judged that Mick was just the kind of bloke that young Les needed right now, and it proved to be a suggestion that both men quickly embraced.

Les was as thrilled to have a bloke like Mick in his corner as Mick was to be in it, and from then on, most afternoons and into the early evenings saw Mick training with Les and another couple of local young boxers by the names of Les

Fletcher and Eric Newton out in the back shed at Pitnacree or in a vacant house down the end of William Street, in East Maitland, which came to be known by the lads as the 'House of Stoush'.

And so the young lads would pair off and punch, moving around a makeshift ring which they'd set up, and throwing and blocking leather as the evening wore on — the flickering candlelight projecting an eerie panorama of ghostly shadow boxing on the walls. Throughout, Mick offered a running commentary of advice.

Left arm up! Left arm up! Good. And again. Block the uppercut now. Block it. Now you're too far forward! Cover up and back up! Back up!

Just how Mick knew so much about the 'sweet science' was never clear — or even, in fact, if he knew that much — but when dealing with lads as young, as raw and as willing as these, even a bit of knowledge was useful. Their rate of improvement in both skill and condition was marked, and bit by bit as they trained, the four became the best of mates — a peculiarity of the sport being that friendships formed fighting were oft' unbreakable.

Eric Newton proved to be a lovely, thoughtful sort of bloke, a kind of amateur philosopher who was very close to his widowed mother, who reflected deeply on things and was always asking Les his opinion — while Les Fletcher was more of a knockabout knock-'em-down and keep going sort of fellow. Les Darcy liked them both a lot, and over time Eric Newton became his best friend — no small thing with a man who had as many friends as Les.

As to the friendship that formed between Les Darcy and Mick Hawkins, that, too, was particularly strong and would survive and flourish even when, not too far down the track winding back, Les Darcy would assume the protective role and Mick would be the follower ...

Ah, but again we're getting too far ahead of ourselves.

You're too far forward, I say! Cover up, and back up! Back up!

At least both Les and Mick were open to new ideas about training, however extraordinary they seemed, and one of these came from a local barber, Con Irwin, who dropped by the 'House of Stoush', and suggested that Les's footwork might be improved if he went along to some of Ted Doherty's dancing lessons down the road. *Dancing?* A lesser bloke might have rejected the idea outright, saying only a sissy would contemplate such a thing, but not Les Darcy. Wasn't he the grandson of Terence O'Rourke, who had so wondrously danced up a storm all the way from Tipperary and then over the Hunter Valley? Why, yes indeed!

Les was light enough of spirit and confident enough of his own manhood that the only thing he cared about was that dancing might help his boxing. (And secondly, no one who had seen him take apart Balser, or heard about it, was likely to risk calling him a 'sissy'. It wasn't that they risked getting a belting from Les for their trouble — for he was not the kind of bloke who ever used his boxing skills outside a ring — but, well, you just wouldn't do it, that's all.)

Next thing you knew, young Les was down there every Tuesday night after training with Mick, learning to waltz, quickstep, two-step, the lot, as Ted Doherty's assistant played up a storm on an old fiddle. Then when he got home, Les would often make the family laugh fit to burst by seconding his brother Frank — whom they all knew as 'Frosty' — to dance around the room, out the door and down the track with him, Frosty near being lifted off his feet sometimes by Les's strength and eagerness. And sure enough, the young boxer's footwork in the ring did improve markedly.

There was a way of moving your feet quickly in boxing which really was close to the way it was done in dancing — always maintaining your balance and poise, based on the endless practice of familiar moves — and Les became all the more fluid around the ring, without yet necessarily knowing the exact best route to take.

It was around this early part of Les's dancing-cum-boxing career that he secured a job as a blacksmith's apprentice with old Bill Ford over on Melbourne Street in East Maitland, for the princely sum of ten shillings a week — a job perfectly suited in terms of the heavy physical work involved to what he now knew was his real calling as a boxer. After all, the famous Kiwi boxer Bob Fitzsimmons, who'd gone on to be heavyweight champion of the world, had always credited his work as a blacksmith with giving him the strength he needed to fight his way through the ranks.

Every morning now, out of bed, up and at 'em, often by 4.30 am, Les would quickly work his way through some morning chores around the farm, and perhaps help his mother get breakfast ready for the younger children, before heading off to be at the blacksmith's by 7 am, dressed in his

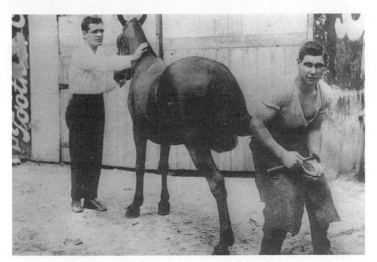
Les Darcy, the 'Blacksmith Boxer'.

grey flannel shirt and leather apron, ready to go. There, going hard all day long, Les wielded the heavy hammer as a striker, while Ford worked the hot iron on the anvil. It was a point of honour with Les to keep driving himself when he was tired, in fact *particularly* when he was tired, and his stamina improved accordingly, even as his physique changed from svelte but muscular boy to a sturdy oak-barrel of a man with powerful biceps, steely forearms and huge, hard hands that were just *made* for striking.

Which was useful, for now around the Maitland area there were opportunities aplenty to expand his boxing experience. Word of Les's talent and courage with his fists had spread clear across Wallis Creek, which separated East Maitland from Maitland proper, and he soon moved up to a better class of boxing ring. There, on 26 July 1911, in an open-air place called the Andrews Ascot Stadium, just behind the Currency Lass Hotel in Maitland, he had real *ropes*, and real *canvas* beneath his feet for the first time — with real carbide flares to illuminate the ring instead of the familiar candlelight! Plus, and this was actually the part Les liked most, he had a more experienced opponent than ever coming at him.

This time it was a highly regarded local fighter who fought under the name of the Donohue Kid, and when Les beat him on points, Les's reputation moved up a few more notches. Of course, it wasn't just the people who saw the bout who were impressed, but those who read the report about it in the following day's *Maitland Daily Mercury*, which had it that both lads 'had all their goods in the window, as the saying goes, and they bustled and slugged gallantly.'[13]

The people of Maitland began to talk about this young fellow, Darcy. Nice bloke, works for ol' Ford, the blacksmith, y'know? He's that happy kid you often see walking around with the sugar bag slung over his shoulder. That's the bag he keeps his gloves in, and he's just about never without 'em!

The bout against the Donohue Kid proved to be a key stepping stone for Les, who now graduated to fighting at the famous Summer Park Stadium in Newcastle, always in front of progressively bigger crowds, for ever bigger purses — and he was never beaten.

Just how good *is* this Darcy bloke? Do you think he might get a chance, fighting down in Sydney? Well, *do* you? The publican asked it of the plumber, who posed the question to the postman, who asked it of the people he ran into on his rounds, and bit by bit everyone had an opinion. Nearly all of the Maitland people now thought Les *was* good enough to fight in Sydney, as did most in the Hunter region, but for the moment there was no offer forthcoming.

It had been such a happy life for Winnie O'Sullivan and her young sister Eileen, and then it had all gone so terribly, terribly wrong. While their parents and older brother had put much of their energies into the oft rowdy Lord Dudley Hotel, these two young ladies had led a more sheltered existence under the firm hand of their father, Thomas, and tight loving guidance of their mother, Sarah. For the most part the girls' lives were filled with school lessons, music practice, religious devotion and the sheer fun of playing with each other. Come the daily pandemonium of the after-work 'swill', when the bar might be lined ten deep as thirsty working men elbowed their way forward to get plenty of drinks in them before staggering home, the girls were usually upstairs serenely doing their homework, practising the piano or already asleep.

And then, in the winter of 1912, Eileen fell ill. While she had been a vibrant little girl, all bouncing with joy, laughter, dolls and dancing, one day the twelve-year-old woke up feeling cold and wan, and no number of blankets, days off school or hot broth seemed to be able to pep her up again. Doctors were consulted, different remedies tried, specialists called in and sometimes there even seemed to be signs of improvement. Always though, there would be a relapse and Eileen would sink to a level lower than any before. The O'Sullivan family — and none more than mother Sarah and sister Winnie, both of whom attended Eileen, taking turns day and night — were besides themselves with worry, but finally all that was left was prayer, as Eileen faded by the hour.

Alas, the Good Lord, in all His unfathomable wisdom, decided not to answer those prayers. And on the afternoon of the 9th of October, 1912, little Eileen closed her eyes and never opened them again. When Sarah O'Sullivan put her hand on her wasted little daughter's forehead to check her temperature, she knew instinctively that Eileen was dead. She and Winnie cried till they could cry no more. Cried as Eileen was taken away to the mortuary, cried as visitors and extended family came to express their condolences, cried all through the funeral, and then at Waverley cemetery, as dear little Eileen was laid beneath the sod. Fourteen-year-old Winnie was torn apart by her sister's death, to the extent that the rest of the family began to worry about Winnie's own health, and as the months passed and things began to resume a certain normalcy, bar the aching vacuum where Eileen used to be, there were still times when Winnie and Sarah only had to look at each other in a certain way and both would dissolve into floods of tears.

Did Les Darcy change in his demeanour, now that when he walked down the main street of Maitland people pointed him out, saying, 'There goes Les Darcy', 'There goes that boxer bloke, the "Boy Boxer" they're all talking about'?

Not Les. Not a bit of it. Never seemed to change at all from the same down-to-earth bloke he always was. He still worked at the smithy, never missing a day; still gave most of his money to his mum; was still the same friendly, fun bloke he'd always been. Sometimes, on the rare occasions when he wasn't working or training, he might be seen riding around East Maitland in the company of his good friend Father Joe Coady — the two of them engaged in deep conversation — but Les never failed to offer a cheery wave and a salutation to those people he knew, which was just about everyone.

A man of the people this Les Darcy, not letting his head get turned by the growing fame and money, but still aiming to be a good smithy when it was all over. But, by gee, now fully formed, he really did look the part of a great boxer. One thing that stood out about him was the extraordinary length of his arms — it later being estimated that such a reach was usually only found on a man who was at least six foot, two inches. Put another way, though usually a fully grown man has a reach from outstretched fingertip to outstretched fingertip which is equal to his height, in the case of Les, that reach extended seven inches longer. Though a much smaller man than, say, Jack Johnson, Les had exactly the same reach!

As it turned out, Les's next opponent, in far and away his biggest fight to date, would be another black American.

For, on 4 November 1912, at Summer Park Stadium, he was booked to fight Dave Depena, a black American who was one of the star protégés of Sam Langford, the black American boxer known as the Boston Tar Baby.

Les had just days before turned seventeen, and was going up against a man in his late twenties who had boxed all over the world and enjoyed something of a minor international reputation. Just half an hour before the bout, perhaps seeking to intimidate the young Australian, Langford took Les aside and confided that Depena was in a mood to destroy him. 'It would be better for you,' Sam tried to advise him, 'if I went in there against you. I's a Christian and kind to kids like you!'

Alas, instead of the panicky, drowning look that Langford had expected from a kid who had just realised he was way out of his depth and about to go under for keeps, he was stunned to see a look of pleasurable expectation break out on Les's face. 'Would you box me, Mr Langford?' he asked. 'I'd love to have a go at you!'[14]

This Darcy fellow really seemed to be different from the run-of-the-mill boxers, and so it proved shortly afterwards, when the fight began. See, as subsequently reported by the *Newcastle Morning Herald and Miners Advocate*, 'Darcy gave a splendid exhibition of the art of avoiding punishment by his clever footwork, timing and judgement of distance.'[15]

After just six rounds, Depena was puffing like a steam train going up a hill, continually jolted by Les's savage short-arm punches, and though the American managed to hold on just a little longer, by the ninth round he was taking such a beating Langford himself tossed in the towel, for mercy's sake.

No one was more impressed with Les Darcy than Depena himself, and after he came back to his senses he told the press that Les was one of the finest boxers he'd fought in his long career. After hearing glowing reports from the north, the Sydney power brokers of boxing, the ones who controlled the Sydney Stadium, were also suitably impressed, and there even began to be a small amount of talk that Les might be given a chance down there in the Big Smoke . . . !

For all that, it wasn't as if all of Les's life was boxing. The thing was, not only was he effectively pursuing his boxing career and copping all the training that entailed, but he was also working something like fifty hours a week at the blacksmith's; fulfilling his role as the almost head of the family; and outright continuing to have fun, by doing such things as playing cards and regaling friends and family with his violin playing whenever the occasion warranted it. With some of his early prize money, Les had bought his oldest sister, Pearlie, a piano, so she could pursue her own musical passion. And then, with the next win, came music lessons for the littlies, which warmed Margaret Darcy's heart, as her own childhood home had been filled with music, and it was wonderful for her to see her own children enjoy it now. Les himself was very good on both the violin and harmonica, and this meant that when he accompanied Pearlie on the piano they could generate quite a sound. Many was the night now that the whole family — usually less Ned, who would be making his own music with a whiskey bottle — gathered around and sang and played until they could sing and play no more.[16]

Girls? Les saw a bit of one called Mary O'Donnell, taking her out to the pictures every second Saturday night, but it was more of a keeping-company thing rather than any grand passion. The two could sometimes be seen out together on a Sunday in a sulky that Les had also somehow found time to build at the blacksmith's workshop. One thing that Les had to allow time for at this point was a quick spell of military training at a camp near Maitland, just as lads all over the country were obliged to do. A decade after Federation, the nation had decided that in these slightly uncertain times, as the British and Germanic empires seemed to be jostling for position, it would be prudent to make it compulsory for all males between twelve and twenty-five years old to learn how to use a gun.[17] Les enjoyed the camp, most particularly because he was able to attend it with his good friends Eric Newton and Les Fletcher, and besides all the digging, ducking, running, shooting and crouching there was even time for boxing! At the officers' behest, the two Les's and Eric put on boxing exhibitions for the other young trainee soldiers.

Whatever his other activities, though, boxing remained his primary passion. In 1913, Les continued to take on all comers, mostly from the Newcastle–Maitland area. One notable exception came when a Sydney boxer who would become one of his great friends, a light heavyweight by the name of Regio Delaney,[18] journeyed to Maitland to take him on in front of a full house. More than willing to tear in on this bitterly cold, wet night in the open Andrews Ascot Stadium in Maitland, Delaney was full of fire from the first, and even succeeded in knocking Les off his feet at one point, before the Maitland man came back swinging so hard, and with such devastating impact, that the referee stopped the fight in the eighth round, and Les had chalked up another victory.[19] With his best payday so far — a whopping £75! — Les, at age seventeen, finally had enough to move the family off Pitnacree and into a house on the outskirts of East Maitland.

This one was a solid brick place on Brisbane Street, with running water. It still had, mind, a bit of a paddock out the back for the dairy herd of seven cows, which had cost up to £15 each, though those cows would have to be taken back daily several miles to the Pitnacree pastures to feed. Under this new roof Les was very proud to be able to get his parents off the corn sacks strung across a wooden frame, which had had to do for a bed all their married life, and onto — tah-DAH! — a real *mattress*. True, it wasn't every night that Ned Darcy was maybe sober enough to appreciate it, but there was no doubt that Margaret Darcy did.

Les continued knocking them over, little or large. One of the most impressive of his fights at this time, at least in terms of making all the locals *true* believers in his worth, was when he fought the famous Cessnock butcher Billy McNabb. Billy was renowned as a terrific fighter, and also boasted a wonderful pedigree, being the nephew of 'Jawbreaker' Jim Fogarty, a great bare-knuckle fighter of the previous generation. (The old blokes who'd seen it for themselves said of Jawbreaker that he only needed one clean punch and he could snap an opponent's jaw clean in two, and there were plenty of fighters of the modern generation who cursed that nephew Billy was equally blessed with that ability.)

On Saturday, 25 October 1913, just six days before his eighteenth birthday, Les fought the 21-year-old McNabb before another packed house in Maitland's Andrews Ascot Stadium — and in a scintillating display, as the crowd howled like a pack of dingoes moving in for the kill, he clearly bested the redhead in a points decision over twenty rounds.

There was, true, a minor setback in his next fight when Les suffered his first defeat, on points, at the hands of the vastly experienced boxer Bobby Whitelaw, who was seventeen years his senior. But there was a very good reason for that — the fight against Billy McNabb had been only eight days earlier and Les's hands were still swollen from banging on Billy's scone.

Though not pleased, Les was straight to the point as he shook hands with Whitelaw at the conclusion of the bout: 'We'll have it on soon, again,' he told him.[20]

Maybe, maybe not. Whitelaw made no reply but was a little more expansive with the press in the dressing room afterwards. After noting how impressed he had been with the young man's toughness, he said: 'He's a great boy, but his handlers should be flogged for putting him up against men like myself. In two or three years, if he's not ruined, he'll be a tough nut.'[21]

In the dressing room opposite, Mick Hawkins was furious with his young charge for having insisted he was up to two bouts in such quick succession: 'You brought it upon yourself, you stupid young bugger.'

Les would not hear of it: 'Cheer up, Mick, the birds will sing again.'[22] And so they would.

Mick felt like slugging him for his lack of worry over the loss, but Les took the view that so long as he had learned from the encounter it was all to the good and, as it happened, Les actually lost very little ground. Certainly, the mighty *Maitland Daily Mercury* didn't think so, as it was now more effusive than ever in its praise — not just for the way Les fought, but for the kind of man he was. 'Darcy is a model youth with his good conduct in and out of the ring,' it reported. 'In private life he is a big, jolly, modest, wholesome boy — full of geniality and bubbling over with laughter and merriment. In addition he is a most loving and generous son to his parents. In the ring his courage is indomitable and his perennial smile and fairness are proverbial. His admirers — they are countless — and the public desire will not be satisfied until they see their champion pitted against one of the numerous English or American cracks at present in this country. It may be said that Darcy is not in their class — but why?'[23] No matter the loss, Maitland backed their boy regardless, and still thought he could be a world beater.

And clearly some of the Sydney promoters were of the same mind, because only two months later, on 5 January 1914, Les fought his first fight in the harbour city, at a newly established stadium at Newtown against an accomplished English boxer by the name of Jack Clarke. The Sydney boxing world was all atwitter at the time for the fact that just four days earlier, on New Year's Day, a 25-year-old fearsome fighter from Wisconsin by the name of Eddie McGoorty, the 'Oshkosh Terror', had fought the now Australian heavyweight champion Gentleman Dave Smith and knocked him out in the first round, with the very same murderous left hook that had also knocked Smith out in the same round, in New York, two years earlier. The swaggering McGoorty was a killer, and there was serious doubt that *any* Australian boxer could hold him.

For Les, this fight against the Englishman was make or break. If he lost his first big fight in Sydney, thus registering two losses in a row, all of the momentum he had built up, all the interest, would be lost and it would take a long time to get it back, if ever. Happily, Les did well, winning on a technical knockout in the ninth round in impressive fashion — with one of the pressmen there going so far as to compare his style with the legendary 'Young Griffo.'[24]

Straight after the bout, Les embarked on what would be something of a pattern for the next few months. That is, as soon as he cleaned up whichever opponent they put in front of him, Les cleaned *himself* up and made sure he got to the bottom of Sussex Street in time to catch the last steamer to Newcastle — from where he could catch the early morning train and would make Mass with Father Coady by 6 am, and then be ready to start work on time at the blacksmith's.

Les knew that, no matter what, he simply *had* to be there, for his employer Mr Ford was a good God-fearing Salvation Army man — who loved nothing better than saving sinners on the streets of Maitland on a Saturday night — and simply didn't approve of boxing, full stop. He would not take kindly to Les being late whatever the reason, and he further thought Les would come to no good by pursuing this 'sporting' career of his. And it would likely mean time off work through injury besides — a prospect that made him even less happy. (Still, Mr Ford could not help but be impressed by the sheer *strength* of his young charge, describing him at the time as 'short, thickset, sturdy of limb, and strong as a little Highland bull . . .'.[25])

The first half of 1914 passed in something of a blur for Les. Almost every month he had a fight, still cleaning 'em up as he went along and making sure that he would be ready for work by the following day. It was not an easy regimen to maintain but it perhaps helped that Les's principal training partners and best friends, Eric Newton and Les Fletcher, were in much the same position. While Les was with Ford the blacksmith, so too was Les Fletcher with another Maitland blacksmith doing equally exhausting work, while Eric Newton was loading the boilers on the steam trains plying the Newcastle–Maitland line with coal. Then in the evenings they would meet to train under the rough instruction of Mick Hawkins, with Les Fletcher and Eric Newton doing their best to match the style that Les Darcy's next opponent was thought to have, while Les tried to work out a way to counter it.

In such a manner the blacksmith boxer bested all of his opponents, including Bobby Whitelaw who'd beaten him the previous November when Les's hands were crook. This time, fighting at the Andrews Ascot Stadium in Maitland, Les won the bout in nothing flat, enabling Whitelaw to sympathise with the poor anvil that had to face the blows of Les Darcy every *day*.

Les was back on track.

2.

Let Slip the Dogs of War

And speaking of damaging blows ...

At 10.15 am on 28 June 1914, the heir to the Emperor of Austria, Archduke Franz Ferdinand, and his wife, Sophie, were in an open-topped limousine bathed in bright sunlight, magisterially gliding down a street in Sarajevo, Bosnia, when a young Serb by the name of Gavrilo Princip charged towards them with a pistol in his hand. Though dying of tuberculosis, Princip was intent on doing his bit for Serbian independence from the Austro-Hungarian Empire before he went, and now fired two shots at the occupants of the limousine.

On the vehicle's running board, bodyguard Franz von Harrach heard the shots, and the next thing he knew a thin stream of blood had spurted from the Archduke's mouth, and had splattered his own right cheek. The Duchess cried out to her husband of fourteen years, 'In Heaven's name, what has happened to you?' And yet no sooner had she said that than she too reeled, bleeding from a terrible wound in her abdomen and she collapsed onto the floor of the car with her face between the Archduke's knees.

Now the Archduke gurgled to his beloved but stricken wife, 'Sophie, Sophie, don't die. Stay alive for the children!'

The bodyguard gathered himself, seized the Archduke by the collar of his uniform to stop his head dropping forward, and asked him if he was in great pain. Franz Ferdinand answered quietly and quite distinctly, 'It's nothing!'

A pause and then he repeated the phrase six more times ... 'It's nothing ... It's nothing ... It's ... nothing ... It's ... ... nothing ... ...' ever more weakly, as his face began to contort. It was almost as if he was trying to convince himself that repeating it would make it so, but it was not to be. Only a few moments after he stopped saying it, there was a violent choking sound caused by the bleeding. Both the Archduke and his wife died shortly afterwards.[1]

The story of the assassination and Princip's subsequent arrest made little impact in Australia at the time ...

In Les Darcy's life, as in the lives of most Australians, the assassination in Sarajevo represented nothing more than a tiny rumble of dirty thunder on the northern horizon ...

What was that?

Something, nothing, move on ...

In the first flush, there were some accounts in the Sydney papers, but it was not considered 'Stop the presses!' material. The account in the *Sydney Morning Herald*, while sympathetic, noted that the Archduke had always seemed a strange kind of chap, from the time he had come on a state visit to Australia in 1892, gone on a hunting expedition over the Blue Mountains, and had no sooner brought some game down than his own retinue of royal taxidermists moved in to gut, stuff and mount them![2] In the *Daily Telegraph*, the initial report ran to no more than one paragraph, and sat right next to a much more important story, given ten paragraphs, about Jack Johnson beating Frank Moran on points in a heavyweight title bout in Paris, a bout chiefly notable because 'many women, wearing handsome gowns, were among the spectators'.[3]

There were, to be sure, in both papers some follow-up articles about possible ramifications of the shooting, but certainly up in Maitland, the whole thing was nowhere near as big as the major news of the day, the thing that *everyone* was talking about: Les Darcy was going to have his first fight at the Sydney Stadium! At the request of the Darcy family, Father Coady himself had gone down to Sydney for a meeting and organised the whole thing![4] Yes, even though Les was still only eighteen years old, it was time for him to make his debut at this stadium, the centre of boxing in Australia, and indeed the southern hemisphere.

These days Huge Deal McIntosh was *so* huge he didn't need to run the Stadium any more, and in 1913 had come to an arrangement with a very well known Sydney identity by the name of 'Snowy' Baker — a former athlete in many fields, including being a silver medallist in boxing at the 1908 Olympics — to run the show. (As to Huge Deal, a fair chunk of the money he made from boxing over the years would go, in 1916, into buying the company that published the *Sunday*

Times, and the most influential sports paper of the time, the *Referee,* making him a very powerful figure indeed.)

First up, Les was billed to box an American, a very curious cove by the name of Fritz Holland. Whereas most of the American boxers tended to come from the wrong side of the tracks with very little to show in terms of refined education, Fritz was notable for the fact that, despite looking like he had been dragged *along* those tracks for most of his life, he was actually university educated, knew how to play six musical instruments including the violin and regularly appeared in vaudeville acts.

And his appearance really was peculiar. That is, just as it had been said that God made the platypus from all the bits he had left over from making other animals, so too did it look as though Fritz Holland had been put together by starting with a student musician with intelligent eyes and then attaching to him every bit of left-over battered boxer that God had handy. This went from the broken nose, to the cauliflower ears, to the gangly arms and rather bowed legs, all the ways back up to the absurd tuft of hair atop his pate, which clung to dear life while all around had receded.

Like most professional boxers, Fritz was in it for the money, and though Australia was a three-week haul by ship away from his native America, it was worth it for the comparatively huge prize money a boxer could earn for himself at Rushcutters Bay. Gosh, darn it, *no one* knew that better than Fritz's manager, the same Tommy Burns who had received such a thrashing at the hands of Jack Johnson at the same venue six years earlier! Tommy was now returned to

Australia as the manager of four American boxers, of whom Fritz was the most accomplished.

Come the night of the fight between Les and Fritz, there was a minor hiccup when the bout was delayed by an hour because the chock-a-block full trains coming from the northern coalfields with 'Les's people', *thousands* of them, had not made it to Sydney as quickly as expected. So did Les fret, fumble or pace the floor to try to alleviate the tension? Not at all — he just sat there quietly, playing some tunes on the harmonica he always had with him, and waited patiently . . .

At last, just before nine o'clock, the latecomers had been seated, the stadium was near packed and the word came to the boxers via a knock on the door and a muffled voice giving them notice: it was time. In the dressing room, Mick Hawkins gave the lad one more bit of advice, and the last encouraging grip on his shoulders. Les looked from Mick to his brother Frosty and then to Les Fletcher and Eric Newton, all of whom had come to Sydney as part of his entourage, and nodded that he understood and was ready.

And now was the hour, on this bitterly freezing July night. Entering the arena proper, there was a massive roar from the crowd at the first sight of Fritz Holland and, in fact, for the man shambling along behind him, Tommy Burns. Oh, yes, they remembered Tommy all right, at least plenty of them did — Tommy, who, in the most humiliating fight any of them had ever seen, had been the great white Receiver-General for black anger . . . Helloooo, Tommy!

Burns, in response, gave what seemed to some to be a slightly sheepish wave of acknowledgement, but no more than that. His focus was on his charge, Fritz, and getting him ready for this fight, not that he expected it would be too much trouble, despite the enormous crowd that this kid Darcy had pulled and the passion they had for him. For, as the battle knell sounded, all other thoughts were drowned as Darcy himself emerged into the light with a posse of three men behind him. At the sight of him, the fight fans, almost as one, were on their feet and cheering wildly.

Les!

Darcy!

Les Darcy!

Some boxers, to be sure, could wither under such adulation, such pressure to perform, but not Les Darcy, never Les Darcy. For now in response to the roar Les waved cheerily, flashed a broad smile — much as he did to anyone who recognised him on the streets of Maitland — and made his way into the ring, attended closely by Hawkins, Fletcher and Newton. Of course there wasn't really a need for all three of them to attend as his 'seconds', but Les just wanted them there, so that was that.

Same thing with Father Coady, who sat in the front row with Frosty. It was not a part of Father Joe's pastoral duties to be there, and he had not attended as a fight fan pure. Rather, he had become extremely close to Les over previous years, and it was unthinkable for him not to be there, just as Frosty, Les and Eric were always going to be in Les Darcy's corner.

From his own corner, Fritz Holland surveyed the scene with an experienced and therefore entirely untroubled eye. There was no way this unmarked fellow opposite smiling at him could beat him, but he, too, had been interested that such a young man could have generated a following enough to fill a stadium this size, and apparently have 3,000 or so more outside trying to get in! How could this be? How could a man of so few years have already developed a following so strong? Such musings were interrupted, as young Darcy's seconds unfurled a large Australian flag ... and now the crowd roared even more!

This patriotic display of the flag started a tradition for Darcy's big fights against boxers from other countries. It had not been the usual practice to date when an Australian fighter took on a foreigner — Australia had, after all, only been in existence as a federated country for a bit over a decade, and the very idea of it had taken a while to get traction. Somehow, though, with young Darcy, it just felt *right*. He was a son of the Australian soil, taking on the best that the rest of the world could throw at him, and displaying the flag highlighted that.

Ask not for whom the bell tolls, it tolls for thee ...

For from the opening bell, Les did what he had always done in boxing matches, which was to charge at his opponent like a bull at a gate, throwing lefts and rights, uppercuts and crosses, in furious flurries that would have completely overwhelmed a lesser opponent. And indeed, Fritz Holland *was* surprised at the extraordinary intensity of the young man. Nevertheless, by simply covering up, he was able to absorb and parry the worst of the blows, smother the charges, and come back with a few hard punches of his own. The key, the American knew, was to weather the storm. There was no way the kid could keep up this pace for long.

But why did he keep smiling? It near put a bloke off to have to punch such a pleasant, friendly countenance, but Fritz did the best he could as Les continued to charge in ... obviously enjoying it *hugely*!

Down in the crowd, Father Coady and Frosty, and not so far along from them, the Australian heavyweight champion Gentleman Dave Smith were watching the clash closely — the latter, as always, analysing every punch, every feint, every move. It was obvious that Les was giving a very good account of himself against this veteran boxer of vast experience, but equally apparent that much of young Darcy's energy was being wasted against Holland's bristling defensive shield.

Though the 27-year-old American really had seemed shocked early at the unexpected thunder and lightning emanating from the youngster's fists, he was nothing if not wily, and bit by bit was able to adjust and make his way back into a fight that in the first rounds seemed to have escaped him.

The spectators, sitting in near-darkness as the two figures went at it beneath the harsh electrical light bulbs suspended above the ring, roared themselves hoarse, trying to *will* Darcy to a great win, but it was always going to be a nail-biter ... No matter how hard Les bored in, the American always seemed to have an answer, a parry, a block, a sharp jab, to momentarily rock him backwards. In the thirteenth round the younger man did seem to get on top but, no, Holland held on and came out almost as strongly in the fourteenth round. True, by the end it was clear that the American was completely exhausted, while Darcy appeared comparatively fresh, but even then Holland was managing to counter most of what his young opponent threw at him and still give back some of his own. No matter, with just a few rounds left in the bout, Les said to Mick Hawkins during the break, 'Gee this is great! I hope it keeps going.'⁵

After twenty rounds of the finest fighting many in the crowd had ever seen, it seemed to most of the spectators that Les was the victor, but the referee and sole judge of the fight — Harald Baker, the brother of the manager of the Stadium, Snowy — was not of the same opinion. And the winner is . . . Fritz . . . Holland!

Fritz Holland!?!?!

Never mind that Les himself smiled gracefully, and warmly shook the hand of the man who had bested him. All around, the stadium went crazy. Boos, hisses, chairs thrown, fists flying, the lot. The men of the coalfield did not take lightly one of their own being called a loser when he *had bloody well won fair and square*, and they made their feelings known in no uncertain terms. Order could only finally be restored by directing fire hoses at the brutes who simply wouldn't quit . . . and those who were trying to set fire to the stadium besides. Even after the police arrived in force, there were still an estimated 8,000 men in the environs of the Stadium an hour after the match was over. Back in the dressing room it was all quiet and Les, for his part, was not at all upset.

The smile he had displayed throughout the fight was genuine; he really had enjoyed going up against such an experienced campaigner as Fritz and, again, felt he had learned a lot. For now the most important thing was to gather himself together and get to Sussex Street in time to catch the

11.30 pm steamer to Newcastle, which would allow both him and Father Coady to make 6 am Sunday morning Mass. And though, because it was a Saturday and Les didn't have to work on the morrow, he nevertheless wanted to get straight home so he could have the early pleasure of giving his prize money — no less than £500! — to his mother.

On the steamer, Father Joe was impressed by the young man's upbeat mood. He had been afraid that Les would be downcast and need reassuring. Instead, Les was thrilled at having fought at the Stadium, against such a veteran as Holland, and having acquitted himself well, without yet attaining victory. 'It's a step in the right direction,' Les told Father Joe, as the throbbing of the small ship's motors propelled them north along the sleeping Australian coastline.[6]

Not surprisingly, Austria-Hungary had taken a very dim view of the assassination of Franz Ferdinand and his wife, and on 23 July 1914 had issued an ultimatum to Serbia demanding it take certain actions Austria-Hungary deemed would stifle such subversive organisations as had nurtured the likes of Gavrilo Princip. When Serbia would not agree to the most punitive of those demands, Austria-Hungary declared war, and on 28 July mobilised its army. An avalanche of agony was soon under way. Just about all of Europe, which for decades had been divided into two blocs of armed alliances, was now drawn into the fray.

Russia, loyal to her Slavic brothers in Serbia, declared war on Austria-Hungary. Germany, allied to Austria-Hungary, in turn declared war on Russia on 1 August. France was allied to Russia and thus had to declare war on Germany, which responded by invading neutral Belgium to quickly get to the ever troublesome French.

The result was that Britain — who was allied to both France and Belgium — declared war on Germany on 4 August 1914. All across Europe, men, munitions and the machinery of war were mobilised — even though there was also a strong worker-led movement *against* the war, with Berlin alone holding twenty-seven rallies in the one day demanding that the Kaiser and the government keep Germany out of it. Those rallies were matched by others in Britain the following day, imploring His Majesty's government to steer clear of a war that seemed to have no overriding moral purpose. Alas, such rallies had no effect whatsoever. In Austria–Hungary, those who spoke out against the war risked execution.

Where did Australia stand in such a dangerous confrontation? As far as the Australian Government was concerned, that was never in doubt. Australia stood, right down to its bootstraps, with the British Empire! That much had been obvious even before Britain formally declared war. Speaking at a political meeting at Horsham in Victoria on the last day of July, the Australian Prime Minister, Joseph Cook, made clear his position in reference to the deepening European crisis.

'The outlook is serious,' he told the gathering, 'and what is going to happen, I don't know. I hope that reason will get the better of these passionate feelings that have been aroused and that there may be peace without resort to arms. We don't know where this fire starts, where this conflagration is going to end and every effort will be made to check it ...

'But, whatever happens, Australia is a part of the Empire right to the full. Remember that when the Empire is at war, so is Australia at war.'[7] Ah, how the people cheered ...

At least, those listening to the Prime Minister did. In other parts of the country, most particularly among the working class and especially the Irish Catholic working class, there was no such enthusiasm. The anti-war view was put most eloquently by the newspaper of the Labor Party, the *Labor Call*, which editorialised that it was 'unthinkable to believe that because an archduke and his missus were slain by a fanatic, the whole of Europe should become a seething battlefield ...' And even more unthinkable that far-off Australia should positively fall over itself to become involved on that battlefield. Just five days later, though, when Britain did indeed declare war on Germany, Prime Minister Cook was as good as his word, and within twenty-four hours committed Australia to fighting beside Britain against Germany.

'It is our baptism of fire,' the *Sydney Morning Herald* enthused, as if to the sound of trumpets, the following day. 'Australia knows something of the flames of war, but its realities have never been brought so close as they will be in the near future.'[8]

Borne along by this sudden surge of patriotism and the desire to fight for what many saw as the 'Mother Country', a lot of able-bodied men from Sydney to Perth, from Darwin to Hobart, began to flood into recruiting centres as of 11 August onwards — to become the Australian Imperial Force, which Cook had promised Great Britain would be 20,000 men strong. And, though within mere weeks there was a change of government, the new Australian Prime Minister, Andrew Fisher, was even *more* gung-ho than his predecessor, declaring Australia would 'rally to the Mother Country' and help and defend her 'to our last man and our last shilling.'[9] Ah, how the people cheered some more. At least most of them did ...

This time, for Les Darcy as for everyone, the events in Europe, clear on the other side of the globe, were far more than a mere distant echo, as the first wave of war-phoria swept over the nation. Australia was at *war*! The pull of it all was certainly strong enough that one evening, only a fortnight after war was declared, Les accompanied Les Fletcher and Eric Newton, after their boxing training was over, down to the local drill hall and all three of them signed the papers that would see them committed to joining the Australian Imperial Force, if only their parents gave their own signatures — as not one of the men was over twenty-one, which was the legal age when you could join without your parents' consent.

Now, as it happened, the again heavily pregnant Margaret Darcy took one look at Les's papers and with great purpose and no little anger hurled them straight into the fire — a confirmation of the clear statement that she had already given her second son that she would *never* consent to him joining up. She followed this with something of a tongue-lashing in such a manner that the little Darcys — Ted, Muriel, Lily and little Kitty — all looked at their mother wide-eyed, as it was so unlike her to lose her temper.

Les Fletcher's parents reacted in much the same way and outright refused to sign. As to Eric Newton's mother, well, it was a close-run thing. Her desire was to refuse, but somehow Eric was so insistent, so *pleading* in the way he begged for the opportunity to join up, that she began to weaken. He was a good boy, her Eric. He had grown into an honest young man whom she was proud of, and a fine worker who would one day, she hoped, be a great husband and father. True, she sometimes suspected that Eric was quietly disappointed to have realised that he wasn't going to be the same calibre of boxing champion as his best friend, Les Darcy — who had become nothing less than the people's hero — but it was not something that had embittered him. And this thing about joining up, about serving Australia, seeing the world, going on an adventure that would surely be all over soon if he didn't join up *now* ... well, she finally felt she simply couldn't say no. And so she signed.

Thank you, Mum!

Within days, after fond farewells Eric was gone, headed off to Sydney to go into camp with the mighty 1st Light Horse Regiment.

Les missed Eric immediately, not just in spirit as his best friend, but physically, as he was obliged to do his training for the rematch with Fritz Holland — now locked in for 12 September back at Sydney Stadium — without his old friend as one of his key sparring partners. It seemed odd, this gap in his training regime where Eric used to be, but if all went well, hopefully his mate would be back with them by Christmas, as the general view seemed to be that the war would not last long and ...

And suddenly, it was time. Only eight weeks after his previous bout, Les Darcy again found himself shaping up to

Fritz Holland at the Stadium, which was again groaning under the weight of a full house and then some.

This time, this time, surely Les was going to put things to rights! *Kill* him, Les!

And yet if Les had improved since his last showing so too had Fritz. No fool him, for this bout the American was not taking the lad lightly and had himself been training hard. This time Fritz succeeded in nearly closing Les's eye in the first round with a massive swinging right, and he knocked him down in the second round. Both times Les recovered to take the fight right to Holland, snapping off a series of straight lefts to the American's jaw, and continuing to fight well for the next eighteen rounds, as the crowd billowed and bellowed as never before, but then it happened ...

Somehow or other — the mechanics of it were never clear — Les hit Holland with such a series of what appeared to be low blows that he was disqualified! One theory was that the wily Holland was in real trouble and had got out of it by rising on his tippy-toes so that such low blows were all the more likely. Whatever it was, the result was the same. And the winner is ... Fritz Holland!

The usual riot ensued, and this time, in the dressing room, Les was more than a bit troubled. 'How did I foul him, Mick?' he asked plaintively. 'How did I *foul* him?'[10]

Again, there was little time to stay and reflect for long as, whatever else, he and Father Coady had to catch the late steamer. Once under way and riding the swell out towards Sydney heads, Les asked Father Coady for some advice about what he should do now. The priest had an answer. His firm view was that what Les most needed now was expert tuition on a permanent basis. Mick Hawkins had been fine to this point, and could certainly remain a part of Les's entourage, but if young Les was going to take on the world he needed someone who had experience at that worldly level and Father Coady knew enough of Australian boxing to suggest who would be perfect for the job. That would be Gentleman Dave Smith.

Dave Smith was a good, decent man, who lived down Mosman way on Sydney's lower North Shore, an oddly bookish boxer, given to wearing a pince-nez; a man of unimpeachable integrity, who had already done much of what Les was seeking to do, which was to become the national champion in his weight class. Most importantly, he had something of a record as a good teacher and had already given Les some instruction on a visit to Maitland. Why not, Father Coady suggested, see if we can't get you out of your indenture to the blacksmith — after all, this trip back to Maitland following fights at the Stadium could hardly go on for the long term — and then move to Sydney and put yourself in the care of Dave Smith? Why not go and train with him full-time? It was certainly something to think about, and Les began doing exactly that before he finally started to drop off to sleep and the tiny ship continued to plough its way north, up and over the unseen swells of the dark night, and onwards to the safe harbour of home ...

Working in the garden of his Mosman home on this sunny afternoon, Dave Smith looked up to see Les standing there.

He had come down, he explained, in the hope that Mr Smith would take him under his wing full-time and teach him everything he knew.[11]

Smith was hugely impressed. This young fellow was already the talk of Australia's boxing community and yet here he was, presenting himself as one who still had an awful lot to learn. And yes, over Les's shoulder at that very moment standing next to a taxi was Mick Hawkins holding two suitcases — wherever Les went Mick went too — but Dave would learn to live with that.

After discussions, Dave Smith and Les Darcy would quickly come to a legal agreement whereby Dave would be the young boxer's coach-cum-manager over one year in return for 20 per cent of the first £100 Les earned, 12.5 per cent of the next £100, and 10 per cent of all monies earned thereafter.[12] To be sure, as Les was still a minor, Mrs Darcy would have to come all the way down from Maitland to sign the papers to make it legal, but from the moment that Dave shook hands with Les on the deal, neither man had any doubt that it was written in stone.

So just who was the recognised middleweight champion of the world? Well, therein lay another tale, one that Les became familiar with as he focused on achieving the title himself. The last time there had been a universally recognised champion, it had been a fellow by the name of Stanley Ketchel who, despite being known as the 'Michigan Assassin', had a particularly close relationship with his mother. In fact, as a kind of psychological trick, before every fight Stanley would make himself think that his opponent had grievously insulted his mother and proceed to box accordingly, with a fury that was frightening. Using such methods and a highly sophisticated form of the 'sweet science' of pugilism technique, he took on all comers from 1907 to 1910, including the famous Boston Tar Baby, Sam Langford, until ...

Until one night in October 1910, Ketchel was on a farm in Missouri training for his next fight when a farm hand by the name of Walter Dipley came around the corner and saw the world champion chatting to his girlfriend, Goldie Smith. Convinced the boxer was out to steal her from him, Dipley took matters into his hands and a few days later, while Ketchel was having lunch, walked up and shot him dead.

A bereaved mother. A murderer in jail. A vacant middleweight world championship. Since that time there had been many claimants, but no one universally acclaimed. The best regarded were Jack Dillon, known as the 'Giant Killer' for his ability to knock out men who far outweighed him, and Mike Gibbons, a fiery middleweight out of St Paul, Minnesota, with a record that also marked him as world class. The *official* world middleweight champion was Al McCoy — who had beaten George Chip in a championship bout that year, though he was often known as the 'Cheese Champion' on the reckoning that he was not really worthy of the title he held, it was just that no one had taken it off him yet. From further afield the French champion and light heavyweight champion of the world, Georges Carpentier, also drew many honourable mentions. The last, at least, was likely out of contention as, amid much fanfare, he had proudly joined the

French Airforce within three days of the war breaking out, and was receiving even greater national acclaim than he had previously experienced as a boxer pure. *Allez Georges!*[13]

If it was a wrench for the still very young Les to leave his family and relatively sheltered life in Maitland and head off into the world unknown, there were at least two things that made it easier for him. The first was that he was now firmly on his way to fulfilling his life's ambition and that was to secure his family's financial future by becoming nothing less than the middleweight champion of the world. Moving to Sydney and training under Dave was clearly a necessary step on that steep ladder.

And the second thing was the sheer wonder of where he was living now. Dave had arranged for him to move into quarters down at The Spit on Sydney's Middle Harbour, into the home of Harry and Lily Pearce and their gaggle of children. Right on the waters of the magnificent Sydney Harbour, surrounded by greenery, was the gym run by Harry where Les would be doing all his training with Dave. It made sense that Les and Mick live with them, the more so because Lily — much younger than Harry, and of a much more generous disposition — was a particularly warm-hearted hostess, a dimpled dumpling of a woman with a belly laugh never far from bursting out. Les adored her from the first, and Lily responded in kind, establishing a relationship that was part maternal — she did all the washing and cooking and scolding of Les and Mick to clean up after themselves and get to bed — and part simply great friendship. The Pearce children also loved Les, and in no time at all he was practically a member of the family, which was precisely the base he needed in Sydney from which to launch his training ...

Every morning Les rose just before the sun and ran in a dead sprint up Spit hill, often passing Dave Smith coming the other way as he walked his dogs in the crisp light of dawn. A cheery wave to Dave, and Les would keep charging on, before finally returning for one of Lily's big breakfasts. That was no sooner digested than her husband, Harry, would take over to put him through a rigorous training regime which would work the breakfast off. And then Dave Smith would take over, teaching Les more of the science and *art* of boxing, usually getting into the ring himself and working through many, many moves, both attack and defence — showing Les the highways and byways, shortcuts and bush tracks around and about the ring that the younger man may have previously not known existed.

While in terms of raw talent Smith recognised that he himself was not in young Les's class, what the older man did have was enormous experience, and this was what he tried to pass on to Les now. How to manoeuvre his way out of a corner when C.O.D. wallops were falling on him from both sides; how to parry a right cross and follow up quickly with a left hook when his opponent's defences would momentarily be down; how to cover up long enough when he had been stung to get himself out of trouble and so on ... Boxing, he made Les understand, had many hidden levels to it, and while you obviously needed an enormous physical quotient to be a champion, you also needed to be able to out-*think* your opponent.

Hour after hour, day after day, the two worked at it, moving around the ring and endlessly drilling feint after fist, punch after parry. Too, Gentleman Dave taught the young man such rudimentary things of professional boxing as to always wrap your hands in thin bandages before putting the gloves on — even while only sparring — and to constantly soak your hands in brine to toughen them up and give your skin the consistency of rough leather. The more you did that, the more punishment they would be able to take before the skin would break, which was where the real problems started.

Sometimes Les's former opponent from Sydney, Regio Delaney, who had now become a close friend, would also stop by and give Les some higher quality opposition for his training. Reggie would throw leather and Les would dodge it before working out the moves to best throw more leather back. Frequently they would do this in the manner of 'shadow sparring', pulling their punches, though other times it was full on. And on and on and on . . .

More often, an American boxer by the name of Jimmy Fitton would take on the role of sparring partner to test and refine Les's improving skills even more — passing on the enormous benefit of his own experience. Les Fletcher, too, briefly came down to give Les some workouts, but soon found the going too tough and returned home to Maitland. No hard feelings, but it was a point of honour with Les Fletcher to do full-on sparring with Les — none of this 'shadow' malarkey — and he soon found that Darcy had moved to a level where Fletcher simply didn't want to be in the ring with him, and certainly not every day. Les Fletcher, by this time, realised that while he might be good enough to be a champion of the Hunter region, the whole Sydney boxing scene just wasn't for him.

And Mick in all this? He was just *there*, pretty much as he always was. Clearly, now that Les had moved up to this level Mick could be of limited use in terms of adding to Les's boxing knowledge. The young man had moved into realms that Mick had barely been able to imagine, let alone have any experience in. And yet when Dave gently broached the subject of whether or not Mick was necessary, Les said flatly that he and Mick were *mates* and that was the end of it. The best Dave could do was to turn Mick into a good rubber so that Les could more quickly recover from their sessions. Dave was also conscious that Mick was a bit of Maitland that Les could have with him wherever he went. This could only be to the good . . . particularly if Les was to take on the *world*, as Dave thought he was capable of.

Other parts of Maitland that had showed in his persona, however, began to fade a little as Dave also applied polish there. For there were ways of moving in high society which Les was not familiar with but Dave was — how to dress for a reception in your honour, how to address a senior politician when you met him, how to wear your bowtie with a certain panache, where to buy a tailored sports coat, and so forth. And the older man was delighted to be able to pass on his advantages.

One thing that didn't change in Les's life was his ongoing commitment to Catholicism and, while living at The Spit, Les did his worship — including weekly confession on Friday evenings and the taking of Holy Communion on

Saturday and Sunday mornings — at Mosman's Sacred Heart Catholic Church, where Father Coady's friend Father 'Ned' O'Brien presided.[14] Always, however, there was the firm focus on building up for the next fight, and what Les was never going to lack for under the circumstances was interest from the wider public in how he would fare. With his many followers having been doubly outraged in previous months that their champion had scored two losses in bouts they felt he had won fair and square, the house was packed to squeaking point when, on 5 October 1914, their Les took on a Frenchman, *Monsieur* K.O. Marchand of France.

Now, normally in a contest between a Frog and an Australian, the Australian would have been the 100 per cent popular favourite, with no sympathy left over for the visitor, but not on this occasion. A short time earlier, France had been invaded by Germany, and so Monsieur K.O. was greeted warmly by the crowd, who expressed in their applause their support for his country at least in these singularly difficult times. Sadly for him, in this bout it was K.O.'s fate to suffer much as his country did against Germany.

This time, despite the fact that K.O. connected flush with Darcy's jaw once in the early rounds, Les gave an accomplished performance. The training with Smith was plainly paying off. Now the young Maitland man was far less a bull at the gate than a surgeon equipped with a dozen kinds of shiny scalpels, and yet only a limited time in which to complete the operation. With a smooth, though still not ruthless, efficiency — for there simply wasn't anything ruthless in Les's spirit — Les moved fluidly around the ring, continually probing inside the Frenchman's defences, and fiercely cutting away wherever he felt weakness. Happily, he found plenty, and in the fifth round it was the Frenchman who was left, like his country, defiant but dazed and unable to rise from the canvas without help. When he came to, he was at least able to say admiringly, 'To fight Les Darcy is like fighting a gorilla. He could beat any middleweight in the world and he could even beat Carpentier.'[15]

Which was as maybe. After another quick trip back to Maitland that night to give his mother the money, Les had a couple of days' break, and then it was straight back into the training ...

3

Heroes

Another day, another gut-busting sprint up Spit hill . . .

Pushing himself now, harder still, legs getting heavier, lungs near bursting, but no mercy. *Nearly* to the top now . . . there . . . and even as the road flattens, so too do Les's legs go from seeming as heavy as anchors to suddenly feeling almost weightless . . . In fact, so near is the boxer to total exhaustion that he can feel almost *nothing* across his whole roaring body, bar the pressing need to keep going, keep pushing . . . knowing as he does that all his senses will soon return as he runs along the flatter Mosman ridge line, and that when they do he will be able to push even harder and go yet faster!

It is a hot day, the first licks of the Sydney summer ahead just starting to caress the shimmering air as the early morning trams take the freshly be-suited commuters in their trilby hats towards their places of work. Out on the harbour the ferries begin to weave their way among some of the bigger ships heading into and out of the port of Sydney.

One of those vessels on this 25th day of October 1914,

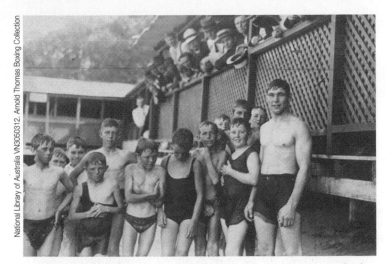

Les Darcy (far right) with some local swimmers at the Mosman baths, circa 1915.

however, is of particular significance to the world of Les Darcy. It is the *Star of Victoria,* a steamship converted to carry the 1st Light Horse Regiment, which had just completed some two months of intensive training, and among the 508 men (including twenty-four officers) and 461 horses on board is Les's great friend and long-time sparring partner *Private* Eric Newton, together with his horse. On the ship the horses are quartered on two decks, making space so tight that the men have to hang their hammocks in the mess.

A few days earlier Eric had had time to briefly return to Maitland to say goodbye to his mother and a few close friends, but because everything was so rushed on his return to Sydney, he didn't have time to go and find Les at The Spit to say goodbye. Never mind. The likelihood was that it wouldn't be long before the two would see each other anyway, and the major fear for Eric and his fellow soldiers of the Light Horse was that the 'fun' would be over before they got there.

As soon as the ship emerged from Sydney Harbour it joined the rest of the Australian convoy containing the first of these troops gathered for overseas service, heading down the coast of New South Wales and then Victoria, before heading west, first across the Great Australian Bight and then the long haul to conquer the Indian Ocean. As far as the troops knew — for they certainly hadn't been told — they were heading to England, via the Cape of Good Hope, which was all to the good. True, there was a certain tedium in being on the high seas for so long, with mile after endless mile of ocean, but the troops listened up closely when a signal was received just four days after they had left Sydney saying that Turkey had entered the war on the side of Germany.

So maybe the war would last a little longer after all. Hip, hip and tally-ho!

Every night, after the day's hard training with Dave Smith, came the fun with the Pearce family. Night after night, any passing rowboat on the harbour would have heard the sound of merriment floating across the waters from the Pearce household, as Les lingered after dinner to play his harmonica or sing or laugh and joke with the children — or just sit around and talk.

Occasionally in these discussions the subject of the war would come up, but not that often. To this point Australian forces had seen no real action and, far from heading to England as the soldiers born beneath the Southern Cross had expected, they had apparently been diverted in the middle of the ocean to land and train not far from Cairo. It was not yet clear where, or if, the Australian soldiers were going to see much action, though some of the smarties who had actually paid attention in geography classes noted that they were now in much the same part of the world as the new enemy, Turkey — so maybe there could be some juicy prospects there — but that was pretty much it. (Some commentators in the newspapers had also noted that the primary strategic threat of Turkey's entrance into the war was that it could move in on the jugular vein of the British Empire, which was the Suez Canal. To forestall that, perhaps Turkey would have to be attacked itself?)

In the meantime Les was delighted to receive occasional postcards from Eric, who, he told Les, had now landed in the Middle East and was training with the Light Horse, just about in the shadows of the Pyramids!

And yet, like most others in Australia, the far-off war was not something that weighed particularly heavily upon Les. Sure, there were plenty of the slightly well-to-do blokes who were keen to fight for King and Country, but there were also tons of common folk who didn't feel like that at all — starting with those from an Irish Catholic background, for whom it usually went against the grain to line up on the side of England in the first place.

With the first flush of enthusiasm for war now faded, the lure of adventure and duty the distant front provided were as nothing to the adventure he was getting in the boxing ring and the duty he continued to feel to look after his own family, first and foremost. His mother, to whom he remained as close as ever, despite their momentary physical separation, had been enduring extended bouts of ill health in recent times, some of which required her going into hospital (quite what ailed her was never clear; its base was probably three parts exhaustion and two parts worry). But her illness — more than ever — made him the linchpin of the family.

Yes, his younger brother Frosty had started work in a bakery, which helped a bit, but after that there were still another ten hungry mouths to feed, not to mention father Ned Darcy's ongoing grog bill. Sometimes Ned would be so blind drunk when he got home that young Frosty would have to call upon the help of a friendly neighbour to get his father safely into bed. When roughly sober, Ned sometimes turned up to Les's fights, and was definitely proud of what his son was achieving, but the old man remained a problem for the entire family, not least the long-suffering Margaret.

All up, it meant that Les *needed* to fight to keep the family going strong. While at this time most of the money he was earning from boxing was going towards buying a big chunk of land in Maitland which he'd had his eye on — with a view to building a house for the family and which he would also fully furnish — Les did allow himself one notable indulgence. It was a car. But not just any car ... this was a Buick, an absolute beauty, with leather trim, convertible top, dark grey chassis and wooden wheels, all with six cylinders and the power of twenty-two horses under the hood ready to be cut loose! True, it set Les back £525 — more or less the equivalent of twenty years' work at his old wage of ten shillings a week as a blacksmith's apprentice — but it was worth it all right!

Motoring now. The wind in his hair, Sydney flashing by, Lily beside him laughing ... For no sooner had he taken possession of the beauty, and got the blessed piece of paper that said he could legally drive it, than they were on their way and Les was fulfilling his promise to take her for a spin around Centennial Park. But suddenly Lily had a better idea. There was no point in having a car like that if you couldn't show it off to people you know, so instead of Centennial Park, why not go to Lily's friends who owned and ran the Lord Dudley Hotel? One of Lily's great soulmates was Sarah O'Sullivan, matriarch of the well-known and well-to-do family, and Lily knew that she would enjoy seeing the Buick and meeting Les, so what do you say, Les? Les, incapable of denying the lovely Lily anything, readily agreed, as for starters he had already met the oldest O'Sullivan son, Maurice, and got on well with him. 'Just one thing when you meet Sarah, though, Les,' Lily said with a twinkle in her eye, 'Keep your eyes off that beautiful daughter of hers!'[1]

Now, quite whether Les was smitten with Winnie O'Sullivan from the moment he met her, or if it happened five seconds later, was never quite sure, but what was obvious was that he was extremely taken with her from the first, and his life effectively changed on the spot. Winnie, just one year younger than the nineteen-year-old Les, was a beautiful young woman with a singularly pleasing spirit. Her long dark hair set off a lovely face, boasting warm and intelligent eyes, and, like Les, she had a very placid, loving nature. Most importantly, she liked Les an equal amount, and the two soon started keeping company — in the physically detached and morally upright manner of the day. Now whenever Les could get time away from his training or fighting or returning to Maitland to see his family, he would make straight to the Lord Dudley Hotel, where he was soon taken to the bosom of a family not at all unlike his own, in terms of being large, close-knit and Irish Catholic. In fact, the O'Sullivan family as a whole so took to Les, and he to them, that now, in the lead-up to fights at Sydney Stadium he would often stay there for as long as a fortnight.

Sometimes Les and Winnie would go to parties together, particularly those at which they could dance and have singalongs. On Friday nights, their favourite activity was to go to dances at Paddington Town Hall, where Les was able to put some of his lessons to good effect — in real dancing, for once! — though Winnie would frequently have to remind him that it would be nice if her own feet could touch the . . . ground. Laughing, he would put her back down, only to swirl her up again shortly afterwards, as a new burst of joy at being together overwhelmed them both. Winnie was as deeply committed to Catholicism as Les, and she would often attend Sunday morning Mass with Les at St Joseph's Church, Woollahra, and there they would pray together.

Beyond all this, Les would also often dine with the O'Sullivan family and very occasionally help serve behind the bar of the Lord Dudley, even though he never touched a

Winnie O'Sullivan, at the age of 20, circa 1917.

drop of alcohol himself. For many a working man, the idea of being served a beer by Les Darcy — getting a close-up look at his biceps and massive fist size, and chatting about his latest fight — was about as close to heaven on earth as it got. Other times, Les would get into long discussions with Winnie's mother, Sarah — whom he laughingly addressed as 'Mum' and in whom he could confide the many concerns he had about his own family — or talk late into the night with the highly educated Maurice, with whom he had developed a very strong friendship. Frequently, he and Maurice would go off on a Saturday afternoon to watch a game of rugby league at the Sydney Cricket Ground, before heading back to the hotel for dinner.

Making the match with Winnie an even nicer fit, Les got on as well with her friends as she did with his. Winnie's closest friend, as a matter of fact, was none other than the vivacious Lily Molloy, an impossibly beautiful young woman with a slightly bohemian air, who had ambitions to be a film star in America!

As for Winnie, she returned Les's affections, though there was one part of his life that she was entirely removed from, and that was his time in the ring. No *lady*, of course, would ever go to a boxing match, and Win had to content herself with staying home and reciting the rosary while Les was fighting, as she waited to hear the result.

Almost always, now, the results were good . . .

On 13 March 1915, Les — at last! — had a win on points against Fritz Holland in Rushcutters Bay, and then followed it up, just to be certain, with another win against him in

Melbourne only six weeks later, where he took Holland apart in spectacular fashion, achieving a technical knockout in the thirteenth round. Les had been so impressive that the likable Fritz commented to the press after the fight: 'You folks think you have a good fighter in Darcy; let me tell you he is ten times better than you think, there is no middleweight in the world he can't beat.'[2]

There were, nevertheless, hiccups in Les's seemingly relentless march to the top of the world middleweight ranks, including two bouts around this time with one of the most highly ranked American middleweights, Jeff Smith, both of which finished unsatisfactorily. In the first contest, Les was giving at least as good as he got, and probably more, only to be felled by a vicious blow to the crotch in the fifth round, which the referee appeared not to see. Infuriated, both at the outrageous foul on his man, and the unbelievable failure to act by the referee, Dave Smith threw the towel into the ring, perhaps way too soon, as it seemed to many that Les could have gone on. In any case, the bout was over, with the only saving grace being that the seeming injustice heightened interest in the return bout. This time, Les pulverised Smith from the first. Alas, instead of a clean knockout, again Smith struck a couple of desperate low blows, and this time was disqualified in the second round — hardly the full-blown drubbing the crowd had been hoping for.

Either way, there was no doubt how impressed Smith was with his opponent, noting afterwards, 'I have never seen a king cobra, but his eyes would, I guess, have a look like Darcy's eyes in the ring. He never blinks, he just glints at you and comes after you. I tried watching his gloves instead: but somehow you get back to those gleaming eyes — and you don't feel so good, so confident, maybe.'[3]

As to Les, after those Smith bouts he still barely had a mark on him. It seemed that Winnie's prayers that Les remain unhurt had been answered.

Praying. Praying. Praying.

For Eric Newton and his fellow soldiers of the Light Horse it was an extraordinary thing to stand on the deck of their troopship in the early dawn light of 12 May and look over to Gallipoli, which appeared almost like a volcano that had received a massive shotgun blast — as it was now belching flame and fire from a dozen places at once, even as tiny ant-like figures scurried all around and what looked like toy ships offshore fired back at the enraged mountain, drawing high spurts of dust in the upper reaches.

Were they really going into the middle of that lot? They were, without their beloved horses, which they had left behind in Cairo after the word had come through that the regiment was urgently needed as reinforcements on the shores of Gallipoli, to fight as mere 'beetle crushers,'[4] as the Light Horse lads called the foot soldiers at the time.

A short time after they landed they found themselves in some front-line trenches in the higher reaches, near a place known as Pope's, just 50 short yards from the enemy. The bullets and artillery fire from the Turks, which went on around the clock, were nearly as difficult to cope with as the dust, heat, noise and, most particularly the *stench* . . .

Dead men in the sun. Mothers' sons, lying in no-man's-land. Bloating. Stinking. It never went away and you never got used to it. Swarms of flies crawled over them, and as the days passed flies would breed and ferret their way inside the decaying corpses, bringing forth yet more swarms to feed. The horror for the men of both sides looking at such scenes over their gun-sights was indescribable, but also a constant reminder as to the likely fate of those who tried to charge, something both sides had tried periodically with always devastating consequences.

On the very early morning of 19 May, it was the Turks' turn . . .

Eric was in the trenches at 3.50 am when, with blood-curdling cries of *'Allah! Allah! Allah!'*, hundreds of them came rushing on, and the only thing you could do was fire into the maelstrom, inevitably bringing down Turkish soldiers with each and every shot, so thickly were they massed. Still, a hundred of them actually got through to the Australian trenches, before being dealt with, mostly by bayonet . . . [5]

It was brutal and bloody, and Eric, sucking in precious air after such heavy exertion, looked around him and couldn't quite believe he had survived it.

Meanwhile, in a spot not so far away, a 22-year-old timber-cutter from Victoria by the name of Albert Jacka was volunteering for the dangerous mission of charging straight at a group of dug-in Turks who had him and some of his mates under heavy fire. When Jacka got there he dived in head-first and succeeded in shooting five Turkish soldiers dead and bayoneting two more. It became the stuff of legend back home in Australia when the news got through. A part of that legend was that when his commanding lieutenant finally peered over the edge of the strangely silent trench the next morning, Jacka was found lazily drawing on a cigarette and said: 'Well, I managed to get the beggars, Sir.'

Jacka won the Victoria Cross, and in an Australia that now had an entirely different definition of what constituted a 'hero,' the Victorian so precisely fitted the bill that his fame was as instant as it was enduring ...

As his own part of the war effort, and acutely conscious that he needed to do something to help, Les Darcy fought frequent boxing exhibitions with Dave Smith in a ring set up on Sydney's Balmoral Beach, just around from The Spit, to raise money for the Patriotic Fund and Red Cross. All up, Les would raise some £70,000 for such causes. He also did his annual three-week stint of compulsory militia training with the Maitland Light Horse. (Though such militia training was not the ideal preparation for a major boxing bout, at least Les was able to spend a good part of it putting on exhibition fights, sparring with his great mate Les Fletcher, as the other trainees cheered them on.)

It was, in fact, while Les was doing that training — then at Largs Military Camp, just north of Maitland — that Eddie McGoorty, the man known to all as the 'Oshkosh Terror', arrived on Australia's shore. The impressive thing was that, even though only a middleweight, McGoorty shortly thereafter knocked out the Australian heavyweight champion, Harold Hardwick!

Les Darcy (left) and Eddie McGoorty shake hands at the Sydney Stadium on the night of their first fight, 31 July 1915.

From Wisconsin, the loud, brash McGoorty was six years older than Les, and consequently vastly more experienced. He was ranked as one of the world's best middleweights, with a notably vicious left hook that had already stopped twenty-eight opponents dead in their tracks. His overall professional record was ninety-two fights for only three losses. The obvious person to put him up against was Les Darcy, who had thirty-four fights for four losses. But Dave Smith, for one, wasn't so sure. After all, he personally had gone up against McGoorty on no fewer than three occasions and had been knocked out by that left hook each time, on two occasions in the first round of the fight! Still, the financial incentives were compelling, and Les, as ever, fancied his chances. One thing in particular, however, made him more than doubly inclined to take on McGoorty.

'They tell me,' McGoorty told the press, shortly after arriving, 'that Dave Smith has a boy he is grooming to avenge my three defeats of Dave. He'll have to be able to take it better than Dave did.'[6] Reading this while still in military camp, Les inquired whether McGoorty himself had ever been knocked out . . .

'Not in a hundred fights,' came the answer.

'Well, let's see if he can take it.'[7]

Thy will be done, gone the sun . . .

With the fight being promoted by Snowy Baker, and an enormous gate guaranteed, it was going to be Les's biggest fight to date — with £750 if he won — and once his three-week military commitment was finally completed for that year, he trained particularly ferociously for the round. In preparation for this fight, Les worked with a variety of sparring partners, though now another one besides Eric Newton, who was no longer available for such choreographed clashes, was his old happy-go-lucky, always laughing mate Reggie Delaney.

Reggie, the professional boxer from Waverley in Sydney's Eastern Suburbs, had decided in July of 1915 to join up to the war effort himself, and was shortly thereafter in uniform, as part of the 2nd Pioneer Battalion, and soon to be on his way to the Middle East for further training, before being deployed. Though it had not been an easy decision for Reggie — for one thing he was newly married to the love of his life, Cathy — he had finally come to the conclusion that joining up was the best option available. A key thing was that it was a certain wage, even if modest, which was better than could be said for his boxing prospects. It was fine for the likes of Les, at his elevated heights, to keep on boxing for the big prize money, but at Reggie's much lower level there simply wasn't the money or the bouts available that there had been. The Newtown Stadium, which had opened with such fanfare before the war, was practically closed these days; the Summer Park Stadium up in Newcastle had closed down; and even the Andrews Ascot Stadium in Maitland, where Reggie had first fought Les, was only hanging on by a thread.

With the news from the front, many of those punters for whom boxing had fed a blood-lust were finding that the times were delivering more blood than anyone could handle, and to others it just didn't seem right to be following essentially frivolous pursuits while something so serious as the war was going on. So Reggie said his goodbyes to Les and his other mates in the now diminishing boxing world, tenderly embraced Cathy, and was gone on his way. Cathy wept, consoled only by the fact that her father was going to be in the same battalion as Reggie, so hopefully whatever happened they would be able to look after each other.

Les trained on.

Finally — in an effort to gather calm before his storm — Les did what he frequently did, which was to spend the last few days before the fight staying with the O'Sullivan family at the Lord Dudley Hotel, resting, reflecting, preparing himself. And yet the old jocular Les was never far away. For, when the time came to head to the Stadium on that evening of 31 July 1915, to leave behind all the familial warmth that he so loved when he was with Winnie and the O'Sullivans and get in the ring with a man who specialised in putting other men to sleep with a single punch, he paused before he went out the door, kissed Mrs O'Sullivan goodbye, said 'I'll be back soon, Mum!', and disappeared with a laugh.[8]

After quickly dropping by St Joseph's Church to make his confession — a practice Les followed before every fight — within a very short time Les was in his rather spartan dressing room at the Stadium, listening to the familiar sounds of muffled mayhem coming from the building crowd on fight night — *for a bout this big they stopped the war, and everyone turned up* — the shouts and cheers and jeers mixing with the clang of distant trams disgorging yet more thousands of punters, even as the pie-men shouted themselves hoarse. This was the big one, the place to be!

Of course, the rest of the world hadn't stopped for this bout, but for the 17,000 spectators who were admitted — roughly 2,000 *above* nominal capacity, with many thousands more left outside — it felt like this was the centre of the universe. And now, there was a different sound . . . the rough, rolling cadence of men attempting to address the crowd. This was, first, a group of wounded soldiers who had just returned from Gallipoli, asking that spectators consider joining up themselves, to replace the likes of them who could take no further part. At the very sight of the men from Gallipoli, the crowd rose to its feet and cheered them to the echo. No, the crowd didn't want to hear what they had to say particularly, but it was the principle of the thing.

Not so kind was what followed when both the NSW Premier and the Opposition Leader climbed into the ring and tried to make speeches with a similar theme. Neither got far before being shouted down.

Get orf! We want the fight! Bring them on! Let's see McGoorty! Where is Les?!

There! Out of the darkness and towards the blinding shaft of white light that had the boxing ring at its base came first Dave Smith, then Les Darcy — *Les! Les! LES! Gunna get him, Les? Gunna belt him? On ya, mate! LES!* — followed by Mick Hawkins, Harry Pearce and Les Fletcher, all of them with faces as grim as Les's own was shining and smiling.

At the first sight of Les, a thunderous applause blew up from the Stadium, a roar that changed only in tone, but not intensity, when Eddie McGoorty made his entrance a few seconds later — *Eddie! Wait till Darcy does ya, mate! McGoorty, you're gunna suck canvas!* — preceded by no fewer than a dozen policemen and followed by his own entourage.

And then it was *on*! Sometimes in fights there is a 'feeling out' flurry in the opening exchanges, as each man tries to work out where his opponent's strengths and weaknesses lie, while trying to show as little as possible on his own account. This, however, was not such an occasion. Rather, right from the first, both Darcy and McGoorty acted as if each had a taxi waiting for him outside and only a limited time to get this thing over with. As the crowd exploded into a frenzy, McGoorty came in hard, swinging heavy blows, but Les was equal to them!

The harder and faster McGoorty threw them, the more Les ducked and bobbed and momentarily back-pedalled, before ripping in with punches of his own — driving them *hard* into the American's ribs and head — as McGoorty, gasping and grunting and throwing off sweat with every one of Les's blows, inevitably had to fall back. Then McGoorty would rouse himself and go again, charging in, as *again* Les manoeuvred with 'a pair of feet as nimble as those of a girl at skipping',[9] as the *Sunday Times* writer put it, to keep himself out of trouble.

Watching it closely from Les's corner, wincing at every McGoorty hit, Dave Smith knew better than anyone the force behind the American's punches, remembering the three times he had been put to sleep by them, but ... somehow, miraculously, Les never really gave McGoorty the chance. For if he was not dancing away from the wild swishes whistling past his ears, he was driving in hard himself, unleashing rips, drives and crosses of his own, constantly battering his opponent, driving his arms like pistons into the American's body.

The crowd roared for more, loving the contest and something else besides ... indeed, they loved Les himself, and the way he went about boxing. As reported by H.D. McIntosh's *Sunday Times* the following day: 'The young Australian's smile is likely to become as famous in its way as Jack Johnson's famous "golden-toothed" grin. In clinches, Darcy takes the crowd into his confidence with an engaging smile that seems to say: "I've got him, got him dead to rights. Just wait and see." The crowd gets the point, too, for it laughs back at the youngster, as though to reply: "All right, ol' man, we knew you could do it." And Darcy gives back an almost elfish grin over his opponent's shoulder. In fact, he smiles from the time he enters the ring till the plaudits of the public, roaring to him across the ropes, proclaim the fall of one more mitt artist before the idol of the hour. When he stops smiling for a moment it generally means trouble for the other fellow ...'[10]

And trouble was exactly what McGoorty was in by the eleventh round. Desperate now, and taking terrible punishment, the American suddenly embarked on a plan which seemed to be to empty both his weaponry and stamina bags of everything they had left in them all at once, in an effort to overwhelm the younger man and finish it. Alas for McGoorty, while this succeeded in bringing the spectators to their feet, it did not bring Darcy to his knees.

At least at the end of one of McGoorty's lightning combinations, a gash became visible above Les's left eye, and the odd bit of blood spattered from it, but it was nothing that Dave Smith and Mick Hawkins couldn't patch up, and into the next rounds Les was as fresh as ever, while the American simply had nothing left to give. In the thirteenth round Les opened up a gash above McGoorty's right eye — rather in the manner of evening things up — and then raised him a smashed nose. Could McGoorty match it again and raise Les one further? He tried. Good God, did he try! For, with just a minute remaining in the thirteenth, McGoorty at last connected with his 'Sunday punch', his infamous left hook, viciously scything in with the last bit of strength he had left in him, and it connected right ... on ... Darcy's *jaw*!

The crowd, stunned, half expected to see Les drop at the American's feet. But not a bit of it! For though the young man momentarily paused, rather the way a bull might if a good-sized apple had been hurled at its nose, twitching his head around a little on his massive neck, to McGoorty's amazement, the local lad did *not* sink to the canvas as so many others had before. Rather, it seemed to give Les an enormous burst of energy ... and intent. He stopped smiling now and started whaling in, reeling off 'left after left that rattled home, here and there, like the viciously spitting bullets of a machine-gun'.[11] In response all McGoorty could do was to try to hold on in the vain hope that the Australian would wear himself out, but by the fifteenth round it was apparent that this was not going to happen. For, from the bell, Darcy came out again — almost as if this bull had been stung on the bottom by a bee and was now enraged — throwing lefts and rights, hooks and uppercuts with equal abandon, nearly all of which were connecting.

Kill him, Les! Finish him off!

The massive noise after that round that was raised from the crowd milling around the Stadium — following the events inside — *had* to be a good sign for those who could hear it from atop the hill at Paddington. (Alas, they could not see it any more, as a roof had been put on the Stadium since the days of the Johnson versus Burns fight.) The fact that the bout had gone this long meant that Darcy was at least *competing* with the American, and there seemed to be a wildly exhilarating edge to the shouting ... which was surely a fair indication that the local boy was on top. At least Winnie prayed so.

And kept praying . . .

At the end of that round, Les returned to his corner, fair cock-a-hoop with the way it was all going, to be greeted by a Mick Hawkins in awe of what he had just seen, the courage, strength and skill that Les had just displayed.

'How going, Friday?' Mick asked the young man, using his favourite nickname for the boxer. 'Pretty good, Old Horse,' Les replied in kind. 'He's not very fast, is he?'[12]

A quick towelling down, a drink of water, some words of encouragement from Mick, and then Les was out there again, seeming to get *stronger* with every passing minute.

With a little time left in the fifteenth round, a savage left from Les sent McGoorty spinning . . . spinning . . . spinning . . . to the canvas, with the referee counting above him.

1 . . . 2 . . . 3 . . . 4 . . . 5 . . . 6 . . . 7 . . . 8 . . . 9 . . .

He's up!

In a display of courage and strength that only a natural-born champion could muster, McGoorty actually got to his feet just an instant before the ten-count was done — though it was soon clear that this was only going to delay, rather than change, the result of the bout's ending.

The famed Oshkosh Terror? This man who had bested no fewer than seventy-five professional opponents, including Dave Smith, Jimmy Clabby, Jeff Smith, Battling Levinsky and Harold Hardwick, now looked more like a just-born baby giraffe, entirely unsure of whether his legs were, or were not, connected to his brain.

The answer was soon apparent, as Les moved in for the kill, and McGoorty simply couldn't move at all, as one crashing blow sent the American back to the canvas whence he had just come, and it looked to be beddy-byes for Eddie.

1! . . . 2! . . . 3! . . . 4! . . . 5! . . .

Again, however, extraordinarily, the brave American could be seen trying to struggle to his feet, but whatever the referee might have to say about it, the Inspector-General of Police, Jim Mitchell, had seen enough, and on the count of five he ordered his men in uniform to stop the fight!

Now, with a roar like that, there could surely be no doubt for those atop the Lord Dudley Hotel, where Winnie and Mrs O'Sullivan had been saying the rosary — *Hail Mary, full of Grace, the Lord is with thee. Blessed art thou amongst women and blessed is the fruit of thy womb, Jesus Christ. Holy Mary, Mother of God, pray for us sinners now and at the hour of our death. Amen.* — just what the result was.

Les Darcy had won, and when Eddie McGoorty at last came back from the land where the fairies flew free and the pixies pranced . . . back from the never-never land where Les had put him courtesy of the first knockout the American had ever suffered . . . he was lavish in his praise. 'That boy's the best fighter I ever fought,' McGoorty told the Sydney press, trying to move his swollen jaw sparingly. 'He's the greatest fighter in the world. He's hard to hit, and harder still to hurt. I don't think there's anyone in the world could beat him.'[13]

And where was Les at the time? Well, the tradition amongst victorious boxers after great bouts was, of course, to head out into the dark night with tight friends and loose women to paint the town red in a blur of blue language, while smoking large cigars and drinking enough grog to float a battleship, but . . . but

Les — a teetotaller who neither smoked nor swore, and who was deeply religious besides — had never observed that tradition. Rather, this night he did what he did most nights after a fight, since he had started squiring Winnie O'Sullivan, which was to immediately head to the Lord Dudley to gather her up, together with her younger brother Jim, and then with other close friends take off to The Spit, where lovely Lily Pearce had prepared a supper of soft drink and cake, and all together they could chat, eat and sing, to the accompaniment of Jim and Les on their violins, while Winnie played piano.[14]

It may have seemed strange to some that the same young man who, just a couple of hours previously, had been all flashing fists and thunder could now be singing and playing with much hearty merriment, but that was just the way Les was . . .

Meantime, back in Sydney proper, those who had seen the fight were simply agog at the skill, courage and sheer *power* of the Maitland lad — *Did you see Les's left hook, his rib-crunchers, his right cross, his uppercut, the way he took McGoorty's best punch and didn't even blink?* — and they talked about it until late into the night. A particularly interested observer of the bout was a colourful American fight promoter by the name of Jack Kearns, who had himself been stunned by Darcy's manifest abilities. (Not quite as stunned as Eddie McGoorty had been, of course, but pretty stunned all the same.) Kearns hailed from the state of Washington, and had come to Australia managing an American fighter by the name of 'Fighting' Billy Murray, whom Darcy was due to fight shortly.

Leaving aside the immediate worry of what Darcy was likely to do to his own charge, what had not escaped Kearns the businessman was the huge following Darcy had been able to generate in a country with such a relatively small population as Australia. How would such a fighter go in America? Kearns thought very well indeed, and it was on the strength of such that he sent a cable to a business associate in America the following day: 'Got my eye on a big one.'[15]

Snowy Baker, meanwhile, had *both* eyes on Les, and all of his fingers on his typewriter, as he sought to capitalise on the young Australian's success by waxing lyrical about Darcy's extraordinary abilities in his regular boxing newsletter, which he sent out to the major American and English newspapers, many of which faithfully printed the extraordinary news along the lines: 'A teenager from Australia had somehow managed to beat the Oshkosh Terror! Fellow by the name of Les Darcy. A blacksmith, just like Bob Fitzsimmons!'

In the NSW Parliament two days after the fight, the Chief Secretary of the Holman Government, the Honourable Arthur Griffiths, was not long in coming to the point. When it came to the behaviour of the crowd at the Les Darcy–Eddie McGoorty fight on Saturday night, hooting the Premier and the Opposition Leader alike when they were trying to speak on the virtues of joining up, words nearly failed him. But he gave it his best shot. 'Among the 15,000 spectators at the Stadium were some of the lowest scum that would disgrace the worst city in the world,' he said. Hear,

hear, said the august *Sydney Morning Herald*, which described the crowd as 'a pack of curs'.[16]

Meanwhile, in Ireland, as Britain started to weaken with its war effort, things were beginning to stir. Was it, perhaps, getting close to time to strike and break the British yoke from their necks? In Dublin the day after Les's victory over Eddie McGoorty, one of the leaders of the Irish separatist movement, Padraic Pearse, stood over the grave of another famous figure in the movement, Jeremiah O'Donovan Rossa, and told the enormous crowd of Irish nationalists: 'The Defenders of this Realm have worked well in secret and in the open. They think that they have pacified Ireland. They think that they have purchased half of us and intimidated the other half. They think that they have foreseen everything, think that they have provided against everything; but, the fools, the fools, the fools! — They have left us our Fenian dead, and while Ireland holds these graves, Ireland unfree shall never be at peace.'[17]

Things were moving . . .

Precisely as Snowy Baker had hoped, interest in Les Darcy began to grow in the United States, and it was Baker's most fervent wish that this would encourage other American boxers to come to Australia to try their luck against the Australian wonder. Kearns saw it differently, though. Shortly after Darcy had indeed cleaned up his own Fighting Billy Murray, the American boxing promoter pulled out all stops to see if he could persuade Darcy to come to America. *Huge* riches, Les m'boy! Great fighters! Wondrous crowds! New York! San Francisco! Chicago!

Something of a tug-of-war then ensued, with Kearns at one end and Snowy Baker at the other, each promoter wanting to effectively 'own' Darcy and have the right to stage his fights. In that tug-of-war, anything went . . .

The lairy Rolls Royce, parked out the front of the Lord Dudley Hotel? The one with the mock snake coiled around each mudguard? That, my friend, belongs to Snowy Baker, and it is proof positive that whatever money there is to be made in the ring, there is a whole lot more to be made out of it, if you have, and keep, the right boxers in your stable. Which is why Snowy is here. See, he is inside right now having a chat to the still frail Margaret Darcy, who is staying with the O'Sullivans for a few days to catch up with her son . . . Baker, a man with a silken tongue, is very polite but very firm with Mrs Darcy. She *must not* let Les go to America with this fellow Kearns, who is a crook, a thief, a charlatan and a cad. Mrs Darcy had to understand just how corrupt the whole world of American boxing was, and just imagine what it would do to a young man like Les if he were so far from kith and kin.

Mrs Darcy appreciated what seemed to be Mr Baker's obvious sincerity but in the range of fears for her son America was not foremost. The war was, and she felt safe to share this anxiety with Mr Baker. 'I'll die,' she kept telling him, 'I'll *die,* if Les goes off to the front.'[18]

As to America, well, Mr Baker certainly did not make it sound good, and she would definitely talk to Les about it . . .

As it happened, Baker needn't have worried too much, at least not then. For the simple thing was that none of Les

Darcy, Mick Hawkins or Dave Smith could quite cop Jack Kearns, this perfumed American with the loud clothes and even louder promises.

After all, in 1913 Dave Smith had had personal experience of going to America on the promise of a fortune, had returned near penniless, and while he had not met Kearns on that trip, he had very much met the type. Now, even though Dave was coming to the end of his one year managing and training Les, and the two were in the process of coming to an amicable agreement not to renew it, the Mosman man strongly advised Les not to throw in his lot with Kearns. The ever faithful Mick Hawkins felt much the same, though for different reasons. Look, Mick didn't have the words to properly spell it all out, but the feeling was the same — he just knew it in his bones that the Yank wasn't on the up and up. Let the Americans come to us, Les. There is no need to go to them.

Kearns, though making heavy headway of it against such an array, kept badgering Les Darcy all the same, bumping up the offer of riches that could be the lad's if he would just accompany Kearns back to America.

Les had never seen it brighter. He was widely acclaimed — if still not officially acknowledged — as the champion middleweight of the world. So great a celebrity was he that a quick-thinking entrepreneur was successfully able to market and sell tens of thousands of badges with naught upon them but Les's smiling dial. Among the proud wearers was even Father Coady back in Maitland, who delighted in putting the badge upon his priestly garb.

They called it the 'Nek'.

It was a small patch of land on the Gallipoli peninsula, no more than three tennis courts in size and, as it was extremely tactically important to controlling a large area around, it was heavily, *heavily* defended by Turkish men and guns in fortified trenches. No matter, it had been decided by the British command that it had to be taken, and they had just the plan and the men — the Australians — to do it. From precisely 4.00 am on the morning of 7 August 1915, and lasting for exactly thirty minutes, a thick naval bombardment would force Johnny Turk to keep his rotten head down, and the instant it was lifted, four waves of the Australian Light Horse — with 200 men in each wave — would charge from their own trenches to the defending Turks just thirty yards away across no-man's-land. They would have no bullets in the chambers of their guns, only bayonets, as the key was not to waste time firing, but to get across the ground and into the Turks! Each man would have a white cross on his back to help identify him in the gloom to his fellow Australians.

There would be a gap of two minutes between each wave and whenever Australian soldiers made it into the Turkish trenches they were to put up marker flags to indicate to the next wave where to aim for. A simultaneous attack by New Zealand from the rear, while other Australian forces attacked another part from the flank would ensure the fracturing of this focus of the Turkish defences. True, there were difficulties with the plan — the Australian war historian

C.E.W. Bean would later say that it 'was like attacking an inverted frying pan from its handle'.[19]

Mere grumbling. The Nek would be taken, no matter the difficulties!

Alas, alas ... Due to unforeseen circumstances, the New Zealanders could not get into position in time. And then the naval bombardment finished seven minutes early, at 4.23 am, meaning that the Turks — fully aware that they were about to be attacked in force — had plenty of time to set up their many German-made, water-cooled Maxim machine-guns, stack their ammunition and bring enormous firepower to bear on the thin stretch of land that separated them from the Australians.

And despite the failure of the plan to work to that point, the British commander of the New Zealand and Australian Division, of which the Light Horse was a part, decided that the attack would go on. In the early morning light, with the sun's glow just beginning to creep up over the Dardanelles, a piercing whistle was heard, followed by a collective, guttural cry.

Up and at 'em, lads!

Almost as one, 200 Australian soldiers, rifles to the fore, bayonets fixed, chambers empty, charged forward, even as the Turkish machine guns began chattering. Screams. Blood. Death. Rising into a solid wall of lead, many tumbled straight back into the trenches whence they came, falling, shattered onto the next group of men getting ready to go out. Maybe a scattered handful of the first lot made it to the Turkish trenches, maybe they didn't. What was certain was that nearly all of those soldiers who had been in the first wave were ruthlessly, easily, cut to pieces by the Turks. Would the second wave of the Light Horse go in?

It would. Two minutes after the first whistle, a second piercing blast rang out. Again, a guttural cry, and again the same result: Screams. Blood. Death. Simultaneously a wave from the 1st Light Horse Regiment — including Eric Newton, boxer from Maitland — attacked from the flanks.[20] Eric was in a wave of another 200 soldiers, of whom 154 were cut down, just as the others had been.

Back at the Nek proper the third main wave of Australians was preparing to go in. Now, from the Turkish lines, came a strange ... *pleading* ... call. *'Dur! Dur! Dur!'* (Don't! Don't! Don't! Do not keep running into our guns, slaughtering yourselves.)[21]

But it was too late. Orders were orders, and the commander would not listen to the pleas of senior officers on site to call off the carnage. The countdown was now on for the next whistle to blow, and, as the seconds ticked by before it went off, one of the Diggers, Trooper Harold Rush, turned to his mate standing next to him, shook his hand, and said, 'Goodbye, cobber, God bless you.'[22] Then the whistle blew, and the Australian wave rolled out, even as the Turkish machine-gunners lined them up and pulled the triggers.

All, all, all were cut to pieces.

Finally, some semblance of sanity prevailed and the fourth whistle did not blow.

At home, the cable came through a few days later addressed to Mrs Mary Maud Newton of Lawes St, East Maitland, Eric's widowed mother.

Regret inform you one-four-seven Private Eric
Owen Newton officially reported missing eighth
August. Any further information received will be
immediately forwarded.

Major Sutton

Agony. Tears. Denial. Hope. Tea. More tears. Prayers.
Hoping against hope. Praying that when she had signed his
papers a year earlier she hadn't signed his death warrant.
Had she? And then, two weeks later, a knock on the door. It
was an upset-looking Father Coady. With him he brought
another cable.

From Victoria Barracks Sydney, to Father
J.J. Coady.
    PR 86 officially reported that number 147
Private E.O. Newton, previously reported
missing, now confirmed killed in action 7/8/15.
Please inform mother Mrs M.M. Newton,
Lawes St., East Maitland and convey deep regret
and sympathy of their majesties the King and
Queen and Commonwealth Government in loss
she and Army sustained by death of soldier,
Reply Paid

Colonel Sandford.[23]

In the carnage at the Nek, it hadn't always been easy to
identify bodies, although in the case of Eric Newton, the
body had a small scar over his right eye, courtesy of a

hard blow received in his early career, which had split his eye open. With his death at Gallipoli, Eric became the hero he couldn't be through boxing — a hero to the people who knew him, and to many who didn't — not that any of it helped Mrs Newton cope with her grief much.

Les too was shocked and grief-stricken when he heard the news from Father Coady. His best friend was *dead*. Eric Newton, with whom he had spent so many hours talking, laughing, growing up, boxing together at the House of Stoush, killed in action, just *gone,* on a battlefield. He could barely believe it. The war had taken on a dimension that no one would have credited at the beginning.

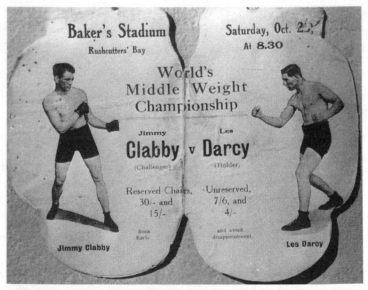

A ticket to the fight between reigning champion Les Darcy and challenger Jimmy Clabby.

And yet even through all his grief, Les was also getting cables of a very different calibre. For now it was not just Kearns who was after him to go to America, but many, many promoters from the United States promising incredible amounts of money if Les would just up sticks and come.

The 20-year-old boxer considered them all, even as he took apart two more high-class Americans in Jimmy Clabby and Fighting Billy Murray again. (The former, when he could talk sensibly again, was able to offer a useful tip to future Darcy opponents: 'Don't hurt him and he'll merely outpoint you. Sting him and he hangs punches on you that threaten to blast your head from your shoulders.'[24])

In the end though, and despite having reached a tentative, informal, agreement with Jack Kearns to the effect that he would go to America, Darcy decided to follow the advice of Dave Smith: 'Stay at home and clean up all the good money lying about. Later when things clear up, you can try your luck in England and America.'[25] So he refused all offers, including that of Kearns, who returned to his home embittered by that fact. After all, he had offered the boy everything, *everything*, and still he wouldn't come!

Trying to ensure that, instead, the great American boxers would come to Les in Australia, Snowy Baker sat at his trusty typewriter. He tried everything, including making the strong claim to American newspapers that Les already was the best in the world.

'According to some of the American sporting papers, the critics are not unanimous in recognizing Darcy as the champion. Can you point anyone out to me who ever gave

Eddie McGoorty a thrashing in every round that he stood before him, and then knocked him out as Darcy did? Will you name me any middleweight who has made Jimmy Clabby look cheap through a 20-round contest . . ? I wish to get in touch with the best class of middleweights to come over here and meet Darcy. If Mike Gibbons makes the trip he can make more money than he can get in America, as can Young Ahearn, George Chip or any middleweight who looks like a champion.' [26]

Alas, at least for the moment, there were no takers.

So from where could the British Empire get the men to replace the likes of Eric Newton, who were being slaughtered or grievously wounded every month?

Exactly. In all parts of the Empire, across the globe, strong recruitment campaigns ran, calling upon the menfolk to do their duty for country and King and *serve*! It is doubtful if any country in the Empire was a more enthusiastic supporter of the war than Australia, with its newly installed Prime Minister, Billy Hughes, himself British-born, who had barely settled into his office in October of 1915 before he was promising Britain another 50,000 men towards the war effort, and was passionately exhorting his countrymen to join up.

On 15 December 1915, he even issued a proclamation, direct from the Prime Minister's office, accompanied by a preliminary enlistment form, to every able-bodied male adult in the country:

THE CALL TO ARMS

The present state of the war imperatively demands that the exercise of the full strength of the Empire and its Allies should be put forth. In this way only can speedy victory be achieved and lasting peace secured ...

The resources of the Allies are more than adequate for this task, but they must be marshalled. To wage this war with less than our full strength is to commit national suicide by slowly bleeding to death.

Our soldiers have done great things in this war. They have carved for Australia a niche in the Temple of the Immortals. Those who have died fell gloriously, but had the number of our forces been doubled, many brave lives would have been spared, the Australian armies would long ago have been camping in Constantinople, and the world war would have been practically over.

We must put forth all our strength. The more men Australia sends to the front, the less the danger will be to each man. Not only victory but safety belongs to the big battalion ...

If you love your country, if you love freedom, then take your place alongside your fellow Australians at the front and help them to achieve a speedy and glorious victory.

On behalf of the Commonwealth Government and in the name of the people of Australia, I ask you to answer 'Yes' to this appeal, and to do your part in this greatest war of all time.

Yours truly,

W. M. Hughes.

Such passion! Such certainty that it was the right thing to do!

It was already rumoured that in order to drum up the extraordinary number of men he needed, the Prime Minister would try to introduce conscription and *force* men to go, but Hughes always hotly denied that. However, his tiny, wizened and rather twisted appearance belied an iron will attached to a Machiavellian soul, and he did succeed in steering through Parliament the *Wartime Precautions Act,* which, among other things, forbade Australian men between the ages of seventeen and forty-five from travelling overseas without permission. For the time being that was where it was left.

Les Darcy and Winnie O'Sullivan were now a devoted couple. So devoted, in fact, that on Christmas Day of 1915, a little over a year since they first began courting, Les asked Winnie to marry him. Alas, such a thing was never going to be possible without her family's blessing and, even though they already adored Les as a son, the O'Sullivans gently declined. All of their experience told them that there would be plenty of time for marriage later on, but it was important not to rush into such a thing, important that the still only 19-year-old Winnie continue her studies, important that both of them gain a little more maturity before taking such a step. When Les asked whether he could at least give her a friendship ring, this was declined too, for fear that people would jump to the wrong conclusion and think it was an engagement ring. So Les gave her a small diamond bracelet instead.[27]

Les was, of course, far too polite a young man to do anything other than accept the O'Sullivan decision graciously, and yet it is possible that Eddie McGoorty himself suffered for it when the two great boxers met again on 27 December 1915, in the Sydney Stadium.

For, this time, in front of 15,000 fans, Eddie must have felt almost as if he was up against a *hurricane* whirling with lead-filled boxing gloves, as — round after round — he was pummelled from all sides by a Les Darcy who was more a force of nature than anything else. Vainly trying to weather the storm, the American kept charging into it and whirling his own arms around, only to be hit by shattering blows that came twisting, scything out of the night and hitting him again and again and again on his ribs, into his belly, onto his arms and straight to his head, *snapping* it backwards. Could he hold on, as now waves of pain crashed all over him and seared around his body, colliding agonisingly in his lungs as, somehow, small sparkles of light seemed to dance around in crazy fashion before his eyes, even while yet more leather pounded in on him, again and again and again ...

And then at last ... somewhere in the far ... far ... distance ... the blessed bell delivered a chance to retreat to his corner where his seconds could roar into his ear — *Left guard up, cover your chin, keep moving around the ring, Eddie* — or was that the roar of the crowd and ... somewhere a bell was ringing and ... he was out there again in the hurricane, leather coming from everywhere, hitting, hitting, hitting, burying him in blows, crashing in upon him and the noise was fading now ... he could hear ringing ... and his legs didn't seem quite connected to his torso any more ... couldn't ... move ... and nor did the punches of Darcy seem to hurt so much as ... wait ... was the whole stadium wobbling or was it him? Getting tired now and ...

And suddenly a towel was launched from McGoorty's corner, tracing a perfect arc through the shattered night above the ring and landing with a terrible finality — *plop* — beside the referee. Call off the hurricane. A technical knockout to Darcy in the eighth round! It was over.

McGoorty, in fact, had showed such guts in the fight, such capacity to take punishment and still not bow his head that the delighted patrons chanted his name when it was all over, but in the bout itself he simply had been unable to find an answer to Les. On this occasion the American had hit the Australian *four times* with the same devastating left hook that had sent so many other men to sleep, and yet not one blow had had any visible effect on Darcy! Les, surrounded by reporters with notebooks after the bout, gave his own summation. 'I am pleased I didn't go to America,' he said. 'Let them come to me, and I will accommodate them one after the other.'

What more could a young man want? Despite the disappointment of not being formally engaged, the main thing was that he had the love of Winnie; he had the unabashed adulation of his countrymen; he had wonderful friends of the likes of Mick Hawkins, Les Fletcher and Father Coady; he had more money than he could ever possibly have imagined; and he was close to getting his family into the circumstances he had long promised himself he would deliver to them. If he really got it right, he could lift the fortunes of a whole generation of Darcys ...

In fact, in the first month of 1916, the entire Darcy brood, twelve-strong, complete with the newborn baby, was moved into the house that Les built — in part literally, because Les had personally done a lot of the brick carting for the builder. It was named 'Lesleigh', and was a beautiful state-of-the-art brick structure on Emerald Street in East Maitland, with a gym out the back where Les intended to do a lot of training when he was home, all of it set on twenty acres of farming land bordered by a swamp. Les had certainly come a long way from the lad who, just over five years earlier, had been so delighted to throw 15 shillings' worth of pennies upon his mother's bed. Certainly, he didn't yet own Lesleigh outright, but he felt confident that at the rate he was going — his prize money for the second McGoorty fight had been £1,000 — it would not take him long to pay back the bank, even though a fair bit of money had to go on paying trainers, sparring partners, taxes and so forth.

But, of course, paydays like that did not happen all the time, and both Les and his key promoter, Snowy Baker, were soon faced with the problem that there really were no reputable middleweights south of the equator that Les hadn't already beaten handsomely. So it was that in something near desperation to come up with a contest in which the public could have some doubt as to the result — and consequently turn up in huge numbers — Snowy Baker moved Darcy up a couple of weight divisions. First Les went up to the light heavyweight division to wallop the Greek American K.O. Brown, and then Baker moved him all the way up to the heavyweight division pure, for a fight against the Australian champion, Harold Hardwick.

Though not a particularly classy heavyweight boxer, Hardwick was a very fine sportsman overall and, apart from being a first-grade footballer with Sydney's Eastern Suburbs Rugby Club, had also represented Australia in the 1912 Olympics as a swimmer, winning one gold and two bronze medals. True, Hardwick had wanted to retire and it took some persuading for Baker to get this genial, big, grizzly bear of a man to do this one last fight, but he finally agreed, and so it was set ...

Right on Harold's jaw.

In front of a ravenous, raving crowd of some 10,000, on the night of 19 February 1916 the unfortunate Hardwick had no chance of withstanding a boxer of Darcy's suddenly beefed-up class and it was all the Olympian could do to stave Les off for the first four rounds let alone try to win the bout. In fact, it was only in the fifth round that Hardwick was able to show anything of his own ability and strength, by firing off one perfect straight left that cut like a cleaver through the stunned night to connect perfectly with Les's two front teeth, snapping them off near the roots. They flew across the canvas and landed just in front of Winnie's momentarily shocked older brother, Maurice O'Sullivan, who was in his usual front-row seat. At the end of the round, Les, bleeding from the mouth but otherwise unhurt, only needed assurance that the teeth had been secured.

Told that Maurice had them safe, Les said grimly, with his bloodied tongue visible through the gap: 'That's the end of the fight then.'[28] In such circumstances it was important to get to the dentist quickly, and so Harold would now have to be promptly dispatched, which he was after another round, falling to the canvas after Les stepped up and fired off some of his own heavier weaponry to knock Harold's block off.

Within mere minutes Les was on his way to have his front teeth re-attached to their stumps with gold pins. In the general scheme of things for the time this wasn't a big deal. Swimmers got big shoulders, football forwards got cauliflower ears, and boxers lost their teeth. It was practically a rite of passage, and Les thought little more about it, apart from advising those close to him, 'Don't tell Mum.'[29] Winnie still thought he was the handsomest thing on two legs and that was all that counted. Too, there was something to be said for the fact that now he was the heavyweight champion of Australia, as well as the middleweight champion.

4.

A Cold Win Blows

Where to next? Who to fight? Exactly.

One possible way of proceeding was to throw in his lot with none other than Huge Deal McIntosh who, though now a newspaper proprietor, still did some boxing promoting if he thought the rewards were great enough. Shortly after the Hardwick fight, McIntosh approached Les with a contract which would guarantee him £6,000 for doing three fights in America, together with a six months' vaudeville tour . . .

Right. While there was no doubt that £6,000 was a lot of money, it was as nothing to the kind of prize money on offer for just *one* fight in America, which could bring more than £10,000 if the bout captured the public imagination and was held in a place like New York. One piece of advice from his friend the boxing journalist Will Lawless particularly struck home: 'Don't sign. Go and get it *yourself*.'[1] After all, it occurred to Les, while sitting opposite Huge Deal, that whatever his own value was in the United States, why did he need to share *any of it* with the Sydney businessman? He wasn't particularly well-versed in the business side of boxing himself, but he knew enough to appreciate that with the contract signed, Huge Deal would simply be able to on-sell his commitment and likely make a huge profit from there. And it wasn't Huge Deal getting into the ring!

So, at a meeting in Huge Deal's well-appointed offices at the *Sunday Times* — with more mahogany and leather around than Les had ever seen in his life — the young boxer gave the powerful newspaper proprietor his decision: Thank you, Mr McIntosh, but no.

Huge Deal was not well pleased. It was rare for a man of his power and influence to be told no, and on the spot he made threats to the effect that if ever Les tried to get to America and do fights without him, he, Huge Deal McIntosh, would do everything in his power to have those fights stopped.[2]

Thank you, Mr McIntosh, but the answer is still no. Les got up, and in a rare display of temper, threw the unsigned contract down on the desk and walked out of the office, leaving a fuming McIntosh behind him.[3] The *insolence* of that boy!

While happy with his decision not to be contracted to Mr McIntosh, there remained for Les a single nagging worry that continued to get stronger as the weeks went by.

The war ...

Every day, the papers were filled with the list of casualties, many of them coming from the unmitigated disaster that had been the Anzac assault on Gallipoli in faraway Turkey, with more than 8,500 Australians killed and a staggering 19,000 wounded. Another 30,000 from other Allied countries had been killed. And all for what? Just before Christmas the surviving Diggers had been pulled out and the net result was that not one yard of ground had been gained! On the streets of Sydney, Maitland and, indeed, all over Australia, more and more people were seen wearing black armbands to signify that they had lost someone in the war. In some ways, those armbands were a badge of bloody honour, and maybe even a reproach to able-bodied men such as Les who had stayed in the safety of Australia. That, indeed, was the view of many, and there was a growing mood that the proper place for the patriot was in uniform, and those who weren't were to be looked upon askance.

The shift in attitude towards such trifling activities as boxing — which had already caused something of a decline, to Reggie Delany's disadvantage — was firming. Letters were appearing in the papers calling for the likes of Les Darcy to lay down his gloves and pick up a rifle!

H.D. McIntosh's *Sunday Times* carried a typical one in March 1916:

> ...take Darcy for instance. It is well known that a strong movement is on foot to send him to America. Is he prepared to go to America to hunt for money at the present time? Is he so devoid of manhood as to lend his support to any attempt that may be made to get him out of the country, whilst all around him thousands and thousands of men with far greater ties in the world are gladly offering themselves as sacrifices on the altar of Liberty? Will the

Commonwealth Government offer this great 'sport' a passport to enable him to run away from his obligations? I hope you will publish this letter or at least make public reference to this cold-footed lot who are staying at home and sham-fighting and making money at the expense of the lives of true men.[4]

Shortly afterwards, the Council for Civic and Moral Advancement called for all boxing stadiums across Australia to be shut down for the duration of the war, on the grounds that they were 'a serious hindrance to recruiting'.[5] Not to be outdone, that well known arbiter of the public good the Very Reverend Professor McIntyre took public aim, saying that boxing 'is a moral blot on Sydney and on the state as a whole. If there was any fighting to be done today, the proper place for it is in the trenches in France where Georges Carpentier, France's greatest boxer, is giving his lifeblood for his country ... '[6]

In such an atmosphere, more and more of Les's friends were joining up, even his old mate Les Fletcher, his sparring partner of so many years — was now heading off to do some *real* fighting. On 20 March 1916, Les Fletcher had signed his papers and was soon training with the 9th Machine Gun Company of the 9th Brigade, which was shortly thereafter to be sent to fight in France.

It was all happening so quickly, with each week bringing more friends and acquaintances suddenly dropping everything, picking up a rifle and marching off. Should Les go too?

It was a question that he continued to ask himself, although there were two very solid reasons why the answer that kept coming back was no.

In the first place, he was still a long way away from securing his family's financial future for good. It was one thing to have substantially paid off his house, but quite another to have enough put aside to tide them through any bad times that might be up ahead. After all, how long could he last as a boxer? It wasn't a life-time job. And secondly, his mother, Margaret, would not sign the documents he needed her to. Full stop. No argument. No nonsense. She *would not sign*. Nor would his father, Ned. And as Les would not be twenty-one years old until 31 October that year, there was nothing he could do about it.

If all of this reasoning might have been sound from Les's own point of view, it changed naught the fact that he would still be a prize recruit for the government, a symbol of the best of Australian manhood marching off to war. The recruitment officials who visited him were absolutely clear. It wasn't him as a fighter they wanted. It was him as an agent of recruitment. If he joined he would receive an immediate officer's commission and be given a job in charge of physical culture.[7]

But still Les would have no part of it. He refused, he quietly told his family, 'to strut around like a prize peacock and be treated as a hero, for acting as bullet bait for the cream of the country'.[8]

So what was he to do in the meantime? The only thing he could do. Keep training, keep boxing, keep hoping that, like one of his opponents, the war would eventually punch itself out, and fade into exhausted submission, that Australia would emerge on the victorious side and things could be as they were.

Of course, things could never be as they were, as Eric Newton's grave alone could attest. And instead of a rough return to normalcy as he had hoped, other events conspired to make Les's own position more untenable than ever.

In Dublin, on the morning of Easter Monday, 1916, some 1,000 armed Irish revolutionaries, led by Padraic Pearse, stormed the General Post Office and other key spots around the city. Just after noon, on the steps of the GPO, Pearse's rolling thunder of a voice rang out over the assembled crowd: 'Standing on that fundamental right and again asserting it in arms in the face of the world, we hereby proclaim the Irish Republic as a Sovereign Independent State, and we pledge our lives and the lives of our comrades-in-arms to the cause of its freedom, of its welfare, and of its exaltation among the nations . . .'[9]

The mobilisation of thousands of British troops to crush the insurrection was not long in coming, and though the revolutionaries — led by the Provisional President and Commander-in-Chief, Padraic Pearse — fought hard, within a week the survivors were obliged to surrender. A few days later, Pearse, with fourteen other rebels, was executed.

Among the heavily Protestant population in Australia, news of the Easter Uprising against British rule — *at a time like this!* — heightened the sense that the Irish Catholics were not really trustworthy members of the Empire and could not be counted on to come to its aid. Instead, they were likely to stab Britain in the back, under their wretched banner of 'Britain's problem is Ireland's opportunity'.

Was there an Australian man more identified with Ireland than Les Darcy, with his companion priest and Papist practices? No! Only Archbishop Daniel Mannix of Melbourne, who had arrived from Ireland just three years previously, came close. It was Les, then, who became a veritable lightning rod for much of the anger extended towards an entire community ...

You see, in Ireland they have the Easter Uprising, and here in Australia we have the Irish Catholics who just *won't fight*, won't join the army, and the worst of the lot is Les Darcy! If he were to join, it might change things, might show that his people had some mettle, and some loyalty to the country, but not him. All he wants to do is box, and make his filthy money, while *our* boys are fighting and giving their lives on the front lines.

Compare Darcy's attitude with the glory of the words of our Prime Minister, Billy Hughes, now on a six-month trip to Great Britain. See the photographs of ol' Billy — with no less than King George and Queen Mary at Westminster Abbey on 25 April 1916, the day that would become known as Anzac Day — and hear his words to our magnificent Australian soldiers from the stage of Her Majesty's Theatre in Piccadilly: 'Your deeds have won you a place in the Temple of the Immortals. The world has hailed you as heroes. On the shining wings of your glorious valour you have inspired us to a newer and better and nobler concept of life; and the deathless deeds of the valiant dead will yet be sung to generations of Australians to the end of time. The story of the Gallipoli campaign has shown that through self-sacrifice alone can men or a nation be saved. And since it has evoked this pure and noble spirit, who should say that this dreadful war was wholly evil, now that in a world saturated with a lust of material things, comes the sweet, purifying breath of self-sacrifice?' [10]

It was just one more speech of many from Billy, who was lionised in Britain wherever he went, hailed as a magnificent leader and loyal son of the Empire, doing so much to provide so many soldiers for Great Britain in her hour of greatest peril. Dinners with the good and the great were held in his honour; he was given the freedom of the city in such places as London, Manchester, Birmingham, York, Sheffield, Cardiff, Bristol and Edinburgh; the Archbishop of Canterbury invited him to dine at Lambeth Palace and the King himself invited our Billy to stay overnight at Windsor Castle!

Glorious!

Disgusting.

Many a day now, Margaret Darcy would go to Lesleigh's letterbox and open the envelopes therein, to find white feathers — the international symbol of cowardice — fluttering out. Aimed at her Les! For Les, too, was receiving the same kind of letters, usually addressed to him care of Sydney Stadium. It was, of course, a bitter irony that the same people who were accusing him of cowardice to go to war were themselves of insufficient courage to include even their names in these letters of loathing. And yet in many ways the letters hit their mark. For while Les could take a left hook or a right uppercut with the best of them, could take a crashing blow to the ribs and barely grunt, the reality was that the feathers did *hurt* ...

The pressure on him to enlist seemed to rise every day, much of it continuing to come from the government's recruitment officers with their guarantee of a cushy job in the army as a physical trainer, and promise that he would not be placed in a dangerous front-line position. He only needed to say yes and come back with his mother's signature. The easiest thing for Les to do would have been to go along with it; persuade his mother, allow the government to so use him and accept the accolades for being a man in uniform. But the fighter from Maitland would have none of it.

'I'll not lead other young men to their deaths,' he continued to say. 'If they wish to go that is their choice, but I wish to have no part of it ...'[11]

There would, no doubt, be many more Australians who met the fate of Eric Newton, but it wouldn't be on Les's say-so. With Les firm in his view that he would not be joining the army any time soon, Snowy Baker at last succeeded in signing him up to a six-bout contract to fight in Sydney, Melbourne and Brisbane — further forestalling the possibility of the star boxer even trying to head to America as someone else's meal ticket. But the lack of serious contenders remained a problem, with other boxers being more than a little reluctant to line up to a pulverising by Darcy, and even if they did, the public had a hard time believing it would be a real contest.

For example, before Les's next fight against the much touted touring Romanian boxer Alex Costica — who was said to have cleaned up most of the British boxers — Costica had to endure the taunts of Coogee schoolchildren as he went on his runs. 'You fighta de Dars . . . de Dars, he kill you!' they called out, in their sing-song Romanian accents.[12]

As if that wasn't enough, one afternoon a spectator made a celebrated comment as he watched the hairy Costica train with a sparring partner: 'It beats me why you're bothering to train to box,' he called out. 'Just practise going down and getting up again; that's all you'll be doing when you meet Darcy.'[13]

In fact, come the bout itself, Costica ended up going down one more time more than he got up, though the usual swarm of police into the ring during the fourth round prevented anything more than a technical knockout being recorded against his name.

Just three weeks later, in front of a disappointing crowd of only 7,000, Buck Crouse — a slugger who was meant to be the toughest thing to ever come out of the famed steel town of Pittsburgh — lasted only *three* rounds against Darcy before he was knocked out. When the American came back to his senses, he nevertheless made an interesting prediction: 'I would stake my last dollar on Darcy against Mike Gibbons at the twelve stone limit, and, great as Jack Dillon is, Darcy at eleven stone six pounds . . . '[14]

Ah, the Americans again. Les, in fact, would have loved to fight both Gibbons and Dillon, not to mention Al McCoy. Gibbons had such fast footwork around the ring that one of his defeated opponents had morosely told his manager afterwards, 'From now on, match me with one guy at a time',[15] while the former farm worker Dillon, named after a racehorse, hit so hard it was sometimes thought he had horseshoes secreted in his gloves. As to Al McCoy, well, he was not meant to be a patch on either of the other boxers, but somehow his strong defensive skills allowed him to retain the title. Not one of them, however, could be persuaded to journey to Australia, and as Darcy was prevented from going to America even if he wanted to — twice now, he had been refused a passport, even though he had offered to pay a £1,000 bond to ensure his return within six months[16] — there seemed to be no obvious solution, darn it all.

Back in 1892, when the famous Australian boxer Young Griffo had decided to seek his fortune in America in the company of some of his boxing mates, the only thing that had stopped him was that he had chickened out while still in sight of the Australian shore, jumped ship, and swum back. Not long afterwards he had got on another ship, stayed aboard, gone all the way and made a fortune! Was still living over there, apparently ...

For now, Les would just have to sit and wait and see what happened.

On the warm evening of 19 July 1916 on the Western Front in France, the Australian 5th Division attacked the Fromelles ridge, at the behest of a British general, for whom it seemed like a good idea at the time. The 5th Division had no battle experience and was not familiar with the terrain, which was defended by overwhelming German forces fully aware that the attack was coming and capable of training both heavy artillery and machine-gun fire on the boggy open fields that the Australians had to cover as best they could even before they began their assault proper.

Lieutenant Alec Raws, from Melbourne, wrote a letter to his sister, describing his own entirely typical experience of what happened in one of the actions that followed:

'I would gladly have shot myself, for I had not the slightest idea where our lines or the enemy's were, and the shells were coming at us from, it seemed, three directions. Well, we lay down terror-stricken along a bank. The shelling was awful . . . we eventually found our way to the right spot out in no-man's-land. Our leader was shot before we arrived and the strain had sent two other officers mad. I and another new officer took charge and dug the trench. We were shot at all the time . . . the wounded and killed had to be thrown to one side . . . I refused to let any sound man help a wounded man; the sound man had to dig . . . we dug on and finished amid a tornado of bursting shells . . . I was buried once and thrown down several times . . . buried with dead and dying. The ground was covered with bodies in all stages of decay and mutilation and I would, after struggling from the earth, pick a body by me to try and lift him out with me and find him a decayed corpse . . . I pulled a head off . . . was covered with blood.

'I went up again in the night and stayed up there. We were shelled to hell ceaselessly. My Company Commander went mad and disappeared . . . '[17]

To a friend, he wrote that although his surviving men were shattered, 'They're sticking at it still, incomparable heroes, all. We are lousy, stinking, unshaven, sleepless . . . I have one puttee, a man's helmet, another dead man's bayonet. My tunic rotten with other men's blood and partly spattered with a comrade's brains.'[18]

Though the carnage described by Raws occurred after the initial assault, at roll call after just the *first* terrible night, the 5th Australian Division had lost 5,533 killed and wounded. Nevertheless, three more Australian divisions were thrown into the fray over the next few weeks, and another 23,000 Australian lives were lost or shattered, including the lives of Lieutenant Alec Raws and his brother Goldy.[19] All over Australia now, men of the cloth, like Father Coady, were knocking on doors and delivering terrible, terrible news.

In the middle of the carnage in France, Lance Corporal Reggie Delaney — newly promoted — did the best he could for as long as he could. But on the morning of 4 August 1916, while in the trenches besides Contalmaison Chateau, near a place called Pozieres, a cruel sliver of shrapnel came twisting, scything from the shattered air all around and hit him in the throat, severing his jugular vein. Great globs of blood burst forth, spurting, gushing out, and it was in vain that his soldier mates tried to stem the flow. Every beat of Reggie's heart saw more of his life blood lost and within minutes his wife was a widow. All his mates could do, even while under heavy shell fire, was bury him a little further back from the trenches, a makeshift cross and his rifle telling where he lay. And that was the end of Reggie.

His father-in-law, 'Teefy', heard about Reggie's death just a little while later. What was he going to tell his daughter Cathy when he saw her again?

If he saw her again. It was getting dark. Still the shells kept falling on the Australians, each burst illuminating a hell on earth as Teefy could never have imagined possible.[20] What kind of madness was it that had brought them here?

Three days later, just less than a mile away, Albert Jacka — who had won the Victoria Cross in Gallipoli — struck again, leading fellow Diggers in a furious charge on some Germans who were taking Australian troops prisoner. Though personally wounded three times in the fierce hand-to-hand fighting that ensued, Jacka won the day in what the official Australian war historian C.E.W. Bean called 'the most dramatic and effective act of individual audacity in the history of the AIF'.[21] Jacka received the Military Cross, as the killing continued all around and his legend grew further.

Billy is back from London! Billy Hughes himself! The great, grand Australian Prime Minister, who has wowed them all, from Westminster to Windsor Castle! Come quick! They're taking him in an open-top car down the main street! They even say he might soon be in line for a peerage, such service has he rendered the Empire.

And so did Hughes make his triumphant return, through the capitals of Perth, Adelaide and Melbourne, with enormous crowds coming to welcome him home, just as they did at train-station stops along the way, singing with full throat: *God Save the King* and *Home Sweet Home*.[22] A wonderful statesman, who has done Australia proud!

For want of any other opponent, Les was obliged to take on his former coach and mentor Dave Smith, who had been lured back into the ring. The first of the fights was in Sydney and the second in Brisbane, with the 'Maitland Wonder', as Les was now known, winning both matches easily. Make that 'fairly easily', for in the second fight Dave cut Les's brow, who returned the favour by breaking Dave's nose in what would prove to be the older man's last fight. Apart from that, the boxing was not of particular significance, but the trip to Brisbane certainly was.

While staying at the luxurious Treasury Hotel on the Brisbane River, Les received another visit from a recruitment officer for the army. No matter that the country had something like 400,000 men under arms at that time, with about 330,000 of them overseas, the authorities were hungry for more, most particularly if they were famous sportsmen. This time something in Les broke, and he agreed that he would join up, even going so far as to appear that very evening — 14 August 1916 — at a recruiting rally at the boxing stadium where the announcement was greeted with great cheers.[23] The following day, of course, newspapers played up the news big, and it became the talk of the sporting world. Les Darcy! He's signed! Darcy has joined up!

Margaret Darcy felt sick to her stomach when she read the news in the *Newcastle Morning Herald and Miners Advocate*, almost as if Les himself had punched her just below the ribs, knocking all of the wind and half the life out of her.[24] True, with baby Joe still on the breast, and young Kitty, Lily, Muriel and Ted all demanding her constant attention, and only Jack, Pearlie and Frank able to provide much help with them and on the farm, Margaret never felt too well at the best of times. But *this*? On top of Ned often being drunk or absent, and her first-born, Cecil, being a cripple, did she now have to face the possibility of Les leaving for the front? What for? To get himself killed with all the rest?

She and Father Coady were in complete agreement that the war was a tragic waste of manhood across the board, and the one solace she had had was that she had not yet lost any of her own children to it, and she had resolutely blocked Les's one attempt so far to put himself in line.

Well, if she had to, she would do it again. Whatever Les had said to the newspapers, he was still under twenty-one and still needed her and Ned's signature before he could sign up. And she just *would not give it*. So long as the good Lord in his mercy gave breath to her soul, she would do everything in her power to keep Les's name off the long casualty list.

The next day in Brisbane Les received a cable from his mother:

Are you mad?[25]

Without her signature it was useless, Les knew it was useless, and now had to advise the authorities to that effect. While the whole episode was extremely embarrassing for him, there was nothing he could do. He understood completely his mother's reluctance to let him go. He was able to take on the world's best with his fists, but his ever loving mother could still stop him cold every time, and he just had to cop the backlash sweet. (Less so, Mick Hawkins. In the face of all the hullabaloo, he made a fairly succinct point to one journalist: 'Darcy is only one man, and can only carry one gun.'[26])

For now there was nothing for it but to leave Brissie and head back to the south on the night train. And it was strange how things worked out. For no sooner had one door closed than another door opened. See, on the train that evening was a bloke Les had noticed around the boxing traps before, one of those people perpetually on the fringes of things while still being in the middle of them — a fellow whose face everyone knew but that was pretty much it. His name was Tim O'Sullivan — no relation to Winnie — a chap in his early thirties who had actually been in Brisbane managing a boxer who'd been in a bout a couple of days after Les's. In the course of this first long conversation the two had ever had, as the Tweed River slipped behind and the locomotive pulled them ever southwards, the subject turned to conscription, and O'Sullivan confided that he really wanted to get out of the country before Billy Hughes had any chance of introducing a referendum on conscription, something that a lot of people had been talking about lately. O'Sullivan, for one, had no desire to find himself in the army.[27]

Funny he should say that. For Les still had hopes of going to America, and it was clear that he was running out of time. If conscription did come in, then that would be the end of it all. Men like him would be put in the army whether they wanted to be there or not, and would have to go *precisely* where they were told to go.[28] And that would be the end of his boxing, and his earning.

The two men kept talking. There might be a way out, noted O'Sullivan smoothly, as *clickety-clack, clickety-clack,* the night fell back. He knew people who knew people who knew the people who mattered in such things and, one way or another, for the right amount of money he felt sure he could arrange to get Les out of Australia and into America.

Les filed the offer away for safekeeping, saying to O'Sullivan that if he couldn't get a passport from the government then O'Sullivan's method might be an option.[29]

Another country, at another time, might have looked at the horrifying list of dead and wounded and turned away — to question whether salvation could *possibly* lie by way of sacrificing more men. Australia, in 1916 under the leadership of Billy Hughes, did not — and the view that predominated in the public domain was that the war was a worthy cause and still the only proper place for an able-bodied Australian man was at the front. Such a view placed enormous pressure on those engaged in so-called frivolous activities that had nothing to do with the war effort — and in those dark days it wasn't just Les who was under the gun to do his bit. Snowy Baker himself was under no little pressure to shut his whole boxing operation down until after the war was over. No matter that sports like rugby league were in full cry, the picture theatres remained open and the last year's Melbourne Cup had been the best attended ever — the particular target of the King-and-country lobby remained boxing in general and Les Darcy in particular.

In an effort to placate the growing outcry, Baker and Darcy met on 24 August 1916 to talk it through. Les made his position clear that, as the all-but-sole bread-winner for a family of twelve, he simply couldn't stop earning and start shooting. And Baker was equally clear: things had to change. Boxing could not go on as it had. The country was at *war*, and boxing had to adapt. In the end, the two came up with something of a compromise measure.

The following day Baker announced their plan in the press: the Maitland Wonder would fight the last of the three fights he was under contract for. After that, there would be no more fights until such time as he had enlisted or the war was over. Perhaps that would settle things down a little . . .

Alas, on the very day that Baker and Les had been meeting in East Maitland, a cable from the British Government arrived in Canberra gravely informing the Australian Government that, 'owing to heavy casualties recently suffered by the Australian Divisions in France, it will be necessary to draw on the 3rd Division for reinforcements.' The only way to stop the break-up of that cherished Australian Division the cable said, would be for Australia to provide a 'special draft of twenty thousand infantry, in addition to normal monthly reinforcements,' and that thereafter for the next three months, they would need 16,500 soldiers per month.[30]

Billy Hughes was adamant. If that is what the British Government wanted then that is what it would get, and after days of discussion with his colleagues he was able to force it through the caucus, enabling him to cable the British Army Council:

> I will send a special draft of 20,000 Infantry immediately, as transport comes to hand, and thereafter 16,500 per month.[31]

There was, of course, only one way that Hughes could fulfil that commitment, and on 30 August 1916, he announced it. In just two months, on 28 October, a referendum would indeed be held on whether or not the nation should introduce conscription so it could provide the manpower the British Empire needed, allowing them to force all able-bodied men over twenty-one to wear a uniform and fight for their country, whether they wanted to or not. The question to be put was relatively straightforward, if cleverly phrased . . .

> Are you in favour of the government having in this grave emergency the same compulsory powers over citizens in regard to requiring their Military Service for the term of this war outside the Commonwealth as it now has in regard to Military Service within the Commonwealth?

In snarling halves, the nation now divided up on that very question. And though there were myriad exceptions, in broad brush strokes it proved that the Protestant middle class was in favour of conscription being introduced, while the Catholic working class, and particularly those members of Irish extraction, was against it — none more so than Archbishop Daniel Mannix, who denounced the Prime Minister's plans in the strongest terms.

'I hope and believe,' he told a packed gathering of Catholics in Melbourne's Clifton Hill parish on 16 September 1916, 'that peace can be secured without conscription. For conscription is a hateful thing, and it is almost certain to bring evil in its train.' Rather than conscription bringing peace, he said, it would simply see a net increase in suffering as the war continued. When it came to Australia's involvement, he had no doubt: 'Australia has done her full share — I am inclined to say even more than her fair share — in this war.'[32]

Outraged, Billy Hughes took aim, again and again, at the Archbishop's words — questioning precisely where his loyalties lay — but this high man of the cloth would not be cowed, and shortly after he went further. During an enormous rally at the Melbourne Town Hall, after it had been announced that Melbourne's Catholics had donated £3,700 to the Irish Relief Fund, which Archbishop Mannix had set up to provide financial support for the families of those shot or imprisoned by the British — the man himself succumbed at the crowd's insistence and spoke passionately.

'My heart bleeds for the suffering Irish people,' he said. As to those who had fallen in the Easter Uprising, he spoke nothing but warmly of 'those brave men who, in the recent rising, loved Ireland, unwisely perhaps, but too well.'[33]

Cry treason!

Billy Hughes was apoplectic in response, and constantly thereafter quoted the Archbishop's words, building the case that the referendum was no less than a fight for the heart and soul of Australia, and something more besides. For Australia itself, the whole continent, was *in peril!* No matter that twenty years before he had argued in the NSW Parliament that 'Australia needs no armies at all, because it is 10,000 miles from danger.'[34] Now, time after time, he sounded the same general theme: 'Germany has long coveted this grand and rich continent, more than fourteen times as large as Germany, and if she wins, she would certainly claim Australia as an important part of her spoils. For this reason, the ramparts of our native land are in fact in the Allied trenches in France. If Britain falls, in Australia there will not be warfare, but massacre. We would be like sheep before the butcher.'[35]

More, Billy, more! And Billy Hughes gave them more, much more. At a campaign rally at the Sydney Town Hall on 18 September 1916 he was at his grandiloquent best. 'To every man and woman in Australia,' he thundered as he reached the crescendo of his speech, 'the appeal of our soldiers fighting on the battlefield falls upon our ears and reaches straight to our hearts. These comrades of ours, those brave volunteers who went through the glories and agonies of Gallipoli and are now gaining fresh laurels in the gigantic battlefields on the soil of France, repose full trust in us. Shall we fail them now?'

'No!' cried the crowd as one, giving the Prime Minister a fresh burst of energy.

'Shall we *condemn them to death*?'

'No! No! No!' came the response.

'For they go to their death unless we send support ... Duty and national honour alike beckon us on ... Who among us will support a base abandonment of our fellow citizens who are fighting for us to the death with deathless heroism ... The nation is in peril ... our duty is clear. Let us rise like men, gird up our loins and do that which duty and self-sacrifice alike dictate.'

His speech finished to tumultuous cheering and applause, which went on until such time as the Prime Minister finally left the stage.[36]

Which was all very well. But against the views of Hughes, many voices were raised. An article in the *Australian Worker*, published by the Australian Workers' Union, for example, put this view: 'Society may say to the individual: "You must love this; you must hate that." But unless the individual feels love or hatred springing from his own convictions and his own feelings, society commands him in vain. He cannot love to order. He cannot hate to order. These passions MUST find their source within his soul ... The man who is forced to fight is as vilely outraged as the woman who is forced to fondle. To thrust a rifle into his hand, and drive him as with whips against a foe, is to degrade him to the level of a dog that is sooled on to attack another.'[37]

Still, however, Hughes was not done. 'We are part of the British Empire,' he roared. 'That is, we are one of the family of free British nations that engirdle the earth. While the

Empire stands, we and all that we hold dear, the many privileges that self-government has enabled us to secure, the White Australia policy, are safe. If the Empire falls we fall with it.'[38] It was clear: vote NO, and the White Australia policy, the only thing keeping the black and yellow hordes at bay from pristine white Australia — the Aborigines didn't count — would be torn asunder. Not at all put off its stride, many in the labour movement maintained that the true danger to white Australia was if all the white workers picked up guns and went away; the only choice then would be to replace them with 'cheap', 'coloured' labour and 'coloured job jumpers'! White Australia would be destroyed.[39]

And so it went: two snarling halves.

For its part, H.D. McIntosh's *Sunday Times* made absolutely clear which half it belonged to and vigorously attacked the anti-conscriptionists for their lack of patriotism. Around the country pro-conscription posters began to appear, one notable one bearing the slogan in big black lettering: **THE WAR CANNOT BE WON ON POINTS — IT MUST BE A KNOCK-OUT**.[40]

Right in the middle of this heated debate, on 30 September 1916, Les took on another American, the former world champion George Chip. Before the bout the hugely influential American syndicated sports columnist Bat Masterson — who, in a past life as a gunfighter in the wild west, with his good friend Wyatt Earp, had been credited with cleaning up Dodge City — had written: 'Chip is the hardest punching middleweight ever sent to Australia and if he lands a clean punch on the Australian blacksmith, another knock-out will be added to his list.'[41]

As it happened, however, it *didn't* happen like that ... For, in fact, the American was added to *Les's* knockout list — after, in the ninth round, Les unleashed one of the cleanest knockout blows ever seen. One who was more than a little impressed was Jimmy Dime, Chip's manager, who told the press: 'Most boxers are strong in one department. Mike Gibbons is clever, Jimmy Clabby is crafty, George Chip and Eddie McGoorty are great punchers — but Darcy has every one of these things and on top of it he's so strong he doesn't seem human. No fighter in the world near his weight could live in the same ring with him.'[42]

And so said all of them ...

Now, even though the crowd for the fight had been a relatively paltry 10,000, the win over Chip was final confirmation — as if it were needed — that if Darcy wasn't the best middleweight boxer in the world, he was certainly right up there. He had, after all, beaten all of Australia's notable middleweights, light heavyweights and heavyweights, and all Americans in his weight class who had a disposition to travel. The problem was that the three men he really *wanted* to fight, in Al McCoy, Mike Gibbons and Jack Dillon, refused to come to Australia.

The obvious thing was to go to America to fight them — and the clamour from the American promoters to do exactly that had never been greater — but the problem was that Les could not legally depart. Just three days before the Chip fight, the Hughes Government had formally knocked back his application for a passport a third time. No explanation was offered. The response was simply 'Application denied'. So was there no other way? What about the whispered conversation he had had with O'Sullivan on the train back from Brisbane a month earlier? The whole idea of it began to work on Les's spirit more than ever.

For, above the riches and chance to prove himself the undisputed middleweight champion of the world, one other thing made America a particularly attractive destination at this time for Les. Put simply, America was *not* in the war. And whereas America remained blessedly apart from the war and no one over there was getting anonymous white feathers in the mail, the situation in Australia for able-bodied men had become progressively more tense, as casualties had continued to mount and the recruits to replace them had not arrived in sufficient numbers. To Billy Hughes's infinite chagrin, there had been only 10,000 fresh join-ups in September, when his target number had been 32,500, so he decided to take extreme action.

On the same weekend that Les fought George Chip, Billy Hughes issued another proclamation to the effect that, from the following Monday morning, there was to be a national call-up for all single and widowed men without children, aged between twenty-one and thirty-five. They would have to report to designated places and assemble in alphabetical order for a preliminary medical examination, where their particulars would be taken and a copy of their fingerprints filed. All before the referendum had even taken place!

Australia was in uproar, with protests, motions, strikes, fierce editorials — and, on the other side, legal prosecutions against all those who would resist the order of the day. What was clearer than ever to Les was that boxing in Australia was coming to an end, one way or another — and the money sustaining his mother and the rest of the family at Lesleigh would dry up. What was the solution?

Phone call for you, Les. It was Tim O'Sullivan. They had met again at a recent boxing match where they had renewed and reviewed their ideas about taking off for America. O'Sullivan was quickly to the point.

Things are beginning to move on the subject we discussed. Will you come out to my boarding house at Randwick so we can talk?[43]

Les would. And in short order the two met and were indeed talking, making plans . . .

Despite the pressure he was under on so many fronts at once, Les kept his chin up, and the absolute foundation stone of his existence was, God bless her socks, Winnie. He continued to squire her around Sydney, remained a constant visitor at her family's dinner table, arriving from his own digs at The Spit, and often took her for long walks around Centennial Park.

It was during one such walk in late October 1916 that he told her, in the strictest secrecy, the momentous news. He was going to America in just the next few days. He'd been contacted by a fellow called O'Sullivan, who'd organised a plan for them to get away. If it all worked the way he thought it would, in just a few weeks he'd be in America and able to fight all the fights on offer, beat the lot of them and come home with enough money to not only set his family up but . . . but maybe set their own family up too, do you reckon, Win?

Once home, he could join the AIF as a soldier, and then everything else would be hunky-dory.

There were tears and tender embraces and an earnest imploring from Winnie for him not to do such a risky thing, but Les's mind was made up. And so it went ...

Les spent the next two days in Sydney getting organised and then came the terrible moment when he really did have to say goodbye to Winnie ... with tears, tender embraces and assurances that it would not be long before they were back together. As to her family, it was simply too risky to bring anyone apart from her brother and Les's dear friend, Maurice, in on it. When the time came to farewell the family as a whole, Les tried to make his departure as normal as possible, with the exception that in the street outside the Lord Dudley he suddenly handed his violin to Winnie's younger brother, Jim, and asked him to look after it for him.

When Jim, surprised, asked Les if he was planning on not being back for a good stretch, Les couldn't bring himself to speak. He simply got in the car and drove away, trying hard not to look back ... [44]

From there, Les hustled back to Maitland. In short order he had sought out his great adviser, Father Joe Coady, and for the better part of an afternoon drove him around and about the Hunter, spelling out his plans even as he gave one last long, loving look at places he knew he wouldn't be seeing for a while.

Father Coady was as strongly against the move as Dave Smith had been when Les had also confided in him. While he understood Les's desire to go to America to look after his family, while he abhorred the government's attempts to sign him up for a war effort he did not believe in, still ... still ... *still*, did Les quite understand the enormity of the step that he was taking? And all of it with a near complete stranger? Who was this O'Sullivan chap? Why take such a chance with someone he couldn't possibly be sure he could trust? Why go against the express wishes of his mother?

For every question Les had an answer. Relax, Father. It will all be fine. I know what I am doing. I am doing this *for* my mother, and my family. I will be back in six months, maximum, after I have fought the fights I want to fight. Nevertheless, in the course of their conversation Les did unburden himself to the good Father, who had for so long been his spiritual mentor and friend.

'Why don't they all leave me alone?' he asked. 'This may be my only chance of a crack at the world title.'

Despite Les's unhappiness at the situation, nothing Father Coady said could persuade Les to abandon the plan, and eventually they, too, had to say their fond farewells, with Father Coady imploring Les to stay faithful to his religion, whatever happened to him.[45]

Les then spent the rest of that final Thursday talking with his family, especially his mother. She didn't understand at all. Didn't want him to go. Why, Les, *why*? Why take such a risk? Desperate, she threatened to call Father Coady.

Les made a firm reply: 'Mum, he already knows.'[46]

Nothing Margaret Darcy could say seemed to make an impact on her son. She would have perhaps felt marginally better if Mick Hawkins — whom she trusted — was going with Les, but Les had decided against it. While personally still very close to Mick, he was following his instincts on this one, and his instinct was that this was a risk he was better taking on his own. Still, Margaret Darcy worried terribly.

Finally she made good on her threat to call Father Coady, and the two had a long conversation. To stop Les, there was only one option left, it seemed to them. That was to tell the authorities. Could they do that? They could not. Les had taken them into his deepest confidence and to betray that would be to totally betray him. They would simply have to pray that he did indeed know what he was doing and that he would be all right. And then, finally, it was time. Time to go ...

He'd be back soon, he promised, and they were *not* to worry. He could take care of himself; this was something he simply had to do. Some final embraces and kisses, and then he moved to the door.

In an instant, Les was gone.

And *stroke* and *stroke* and *stroke*. Carefully, quietly, floating phantoms on the water, gliding to their goal.

Every tug of the oar into the moonlit Newcastle harbour took the rowboat bearing Les Darcy and Tim O'Sullivan further from the Australian shore and towards the dark, looming presence that was the *Hattie Luckenbach,* a small collier with thirty-odd crew that was about to take coals from Newcastle ... to South America. All remained quiet on the ship as they clambered up its side, to be met by a furtive figure who emerged from the shadows, took O'Sullivan's proffered bag of gold sovereigns, and silently bade them to follow him.

With barely a word spoken they were taken down into the very bowels of the ship — dark, airless and pressing — where they were hidden under some sails deep within the hold.

An extraordinarily hot and uncomfortable night followed but, at least, at last, the throb of the engines and vibration of the propeller shaft, which was just yards away from where they lay ensconced, told them that they were under way. Australia was now falling behind with every turn of the propeller.

Saturday 28 October 1916 dawned hot and warm across most of Australia, as the nation at last went to the polls to cast their vote on whether the government should, or should not, have the right to force a man to carry a gun and go overseas to war, once they turned twenty-one. Up in East Maitland, both Margaret Darcy and Father Coady voted, and both were firm in putting the cross in the box for NO. Both, however, were of heavy heart, each wondering just how Les was getting on, where he was, what was happening, and most particularly, would he be all right?

The thing about seasickness, they say, is that in the first twelve hours you're afraid you're going to die, and in the next twelve hours you're afraid you're *not* going to die. In that first dreadful day on the ship out in the open sea, both Les Darcy and Tim O'Sullivan did it extremely tough. In the heavy swell both men parted with every meal they'd had in recent times. They simply could not keep down the meagre provisions they'd brought with them. It was thus a great moment on the Saturday when, now safely in international waters and far enough out to sea that there could be no turning back, they were able to declare themselves to the captain, a grizzled Scot by the name of Jas McDonald.

Hello, we're stowaways on your fine vessel. Les introduced himself as Mr Dawson, O'Sullivan as Mr Edwards. Both men had taken care to remove all tags and identification from their personal effects before boarding the ship, so there was certainly nothing to contradict their statements. And in fact, as part of the money Les had handed over was going to McDonald — and he had been in on the deal from the first — the amazement the skipper evinced was feigned for the benefit of the crew, as was his perfunctory dressing down of the first mate for not having done a thorough enough search when the ship departed.

Following standard practice in such situations, the two were immediately put to work as stokers, until such times as the ship reached its destination.

Billy Hughes had his answer: NO.

By a narrow margin, Australians had denied the government the right to force men to fight against their will. The national call-up, which had been going at full throttle, was called off, and those who were being prosecuted for their lack of co-operation had all charges dropped. For the moment the situation settled down, at least a little. Had Les Darcy still been in Australia he would have been free to go about his business without being forced to join up.

Ah, but was he?

Have you heard?

Les! Les Darcy! He's scarpered! Gone! Stowed away on a ship bound for America, and taken off!

The news that Les Darcy had left Australia was extraordinary, indeed, and it first began to break on the Monday after he had left. That morning W.F. Corbett, the sports editor of the *Referee*, received a curious phone call from Snowy Baker.[47] The boxing impresario told Corbett that he had, in turn, just taken a phone call from someone saying that Darcy had stowed away on a ship going to America, and that Corbett had gone as his manager! Corbett quickly assured him that this was not the case, as witness his continued presence in Australia. But from that point on there was no holding the news.

Shortly afterwards, the *Referee* led with the story . . .

SYDNEY BOXING MYSTERY
Where Is Our Boxing Champion?

. . . and floated the story that Les was afloat himself at that very moment, and heading east.

The *Melbourne Herald* was also on the case, on the same day:

DARCY MISSING
Boxer Said to Have Left on Tramp Steamer for USA
Tempted by Big Offers

If the tone of those stories was more stunned than condemnatory, it didn't take long for the mood to change — once Darcy's departure was confirmed — led by withering blasts from both Huge Deal McIntosh and Snowy Baker, who'd lost their primary meal-ticket. Baker quickly put out a statement that went to both Australian and American newspapers, containing the key line:

> Owing to Les Darcy's unpatriotic action in clearing out from his country, at a time when he should be doing his bit with his Australian comrades, it has been decided to strip him of his middleweight and heavyweight championship titles.[48]

Not content with that, McIntosh wanted Les stripped of all his earthly goods as well, with his *Sunday Times* newspaper accusing Darcy of everything but stealing chickens and causing the drought.

Under the blaring headline:

COLD-FOOTED LES DARCY
Bolts From Australia
to Escape Home Defence
Government Should Seize His Property

the paper took direct aim at the same man it had previously lionised.

'Now it seems to be definitely established that Les Darcy has slipped away to America, this paper and a great crowd of reputable citizens want to know what action the Federal government proposes taking in the matter. Here is a young man in the heyday of his physical fitness, the most able-bodied athlete in the Commonwealth, middleweight champion of the world, as well as heavyweight champion of Australia, whose annual income for the past three years has not been less than £5,000.

'He is fit for military service and he has made all this money out of the people of Australia. Australia has put him into a position of advantage that few young Australian men at this crisis enjoy; he is independent for life, if need be, and in case of his death his parents are abundantly well provided for.

'All this Australia has done for Les Darcy. What has Les Darcy done for Australia? He has turned tail and made a bolt for it the moment when it seemed that he could no longer dodge his plain duty to the country that has fed and pampered him. The Commonwealth Government surely cannot sit down meekly and submit to the indignity of this man's lawlessness and breach of common faith. Is there not some way in which the government can seize his property?'

Precisely on what legal grounds the government could have done so were not made clear — after all, the only law Darcy had broken was to have left Australia without a proper passport tucked into his top pocket, but Huge Deal's paper did not concern itself with such niceties. In fact, it went even further, seriously advocating that the government pursue him overseas. For it went on: 'The Commonwealth might reasonably request that the United States will refuse permission to Darcy to land. He can be barred quite easily as an undesirable immigrant. If you can conceive an immigrant more undesirable than a disloyal pugilist with a yellow streak, your imagination is fine.'

True, there was a minor problem when, shortly after this diatribe appeared, Sydney's *Mirror* reprinted an article from the *New York Police Gazette* which gave a blow-by-blow account of the proposal put by Huge Deal McIntosh to take Darcy to America himself, but after Huge Deal threatened legal Armageddon if they did not retract, the paper did precisely that, publishing a grovelling apology and asserting that the story had no foundation whatsoever and they simply didn't know what had come over them to have printed it. Normal service was then resumed, with Darcy now always the target and, if you didn't know better, you might have thought the boxer was just about the only man in all of Australia who was not inclined to join the AIF.

Of course, he was not. All over Australia, men, for their own reasons — including the fact that they were the chief breadwinners for their family — were declining to go. One of these was none other than the young Robert Menzies, who would go on to be the Prime Minister, but at the time the flak he took was almost none. For Menzies was not famous enough to be a symbol.

At least some voices were raised in defence of Les, however, and none was more eloquent than a writer for the *Daily Mirror,* whose words appeared beneath the headline:

What Has Darcy Done?

He wrote: 'For some peculiar reason or another, quite a number of persons are, or pretend to be, interested in the movements of the boxer Les Darcy. The interest of the bulk of these persons is centred on seeing Darcy become a soldier. The fact that Darcy may hold other views over the disposal of his life cuts no ice with these warriors by proxy. Having decided that Darcy should be a soldier, any delay on his part to oblige them is looked upon as a personal injury ... '[49]

Of course, Mick Hawkins also remained faithful, though he, too, had been hurt by the manner of Les's departure, and that his great friend had not taken him into his confidence before leaving, or even given him a chance to talk him out of it. What particularly hurt was that Les had gone with this fellow O'Sullivan, whom they'd met on the train back from Brisbane. Mick hadn't liked the look of him from the first.

'Take my tip,' Mick said to the journalist W.F. Corbett shortly after Les had departed. 'Darcy will drop that fellow he has with him, directly they reach America. He won't be handicapped by anybody. When we met with him in Brisbane and other places Les asked me what sort of chap he was, and what he did. I could not say much about the man ... I wish the boy well, but I would have preferred to see him go away under more favourable conditions.'[50]

Of them all, it was probably the Brisbane *Courier-Mail* which most outdid itself with an open letter to Les that simply dripped with loathing:

'Your twenty-first birthday found you, the great Les Darcy, the marvellous fighter, the Australian bulldog, on board a miserable tinpot vessel, fleeing in disguise from the land where they fight for love to the land where they skite for money; all because you THOUGHT they were going to make you stand in line with such second-raters as Corporal

Jacka, Corporal Dunstan, Georges Carpentier and others in the great army of liberty.

'You are the most striking example that we could possibly hold up out of tens of thousands of men who could go, but won't go to the front and fight for Australia.'[51]

Why such extraordinary vitriol, and against almost Les alone? A recent census had shown that there were no fewer than 200,000 men in Australia who were able-bodied but had not signed up, among whom were none other than Snowy Baker and Hugh D. McIntosh. Both of them were young enough, at thirty-two and forty years of age respectively, to join up, and yet neither had been seen fit to put his own hand up and snap off a salute — 'Reporting for duty, SIR!'

Up in East Maitland at Lesleigh, such newspaper articles caused enormous distress, compounded by the letters that now started to *flood* in, as ever penned anonymously, accusing Les Darcy of being a coward. Many of them, his mother noticed with bitterness, had East Maitland markings, meaning they had come from people in the neighbourhood.

Down in Paddington there was equal anxiety at what was being written about Les — and it was so bad that Winnie's father, Thomas, specifically forbade her to read the papers for fear that she would make herself ill with distress.

Winnie missed Les terribly and continued to write to him every day, care of a contact address Les had given her in America, so that when he did arrive it would at least not be long before he received her news and love from home.

5

America

Out on the high seas Les sailed on, oblivious to the treatment he was receiving at home. At one point, perhaps with wry amusement, the captain of the *Hattie Luckenbach* suggested it might be in order to have a few bouts of boxing on the deck with a couple of his sailors who fancied themselves as keen exponents of pugilism even though they had no idea who Les truly was. Les happily obliged, though it wasn't long before those sailors decided they weren't quite as good as they had thought.

The torpor of the tropics was briefly interrupted when the collier was boarded by mariners from a German submarine who were ensuring that it was carrying no munitions, but apart from that, all was relatively calm on board. Les wrote a few letters, did as much exercise as he could to stay fit within the confines of the ship, running up and down the metal stairs and doing some exercises on the deck, though mostly he just waited until they could make port. The first stop came in South America, in Chile in fact, where, after firing off a cable to a New York boxing promoter by the name of Tex Rickard — informing him of their estimated time and mode of arrival — he and Tim O'Sullivan changed ships, now boarding the SS *Cushing*. After making their way through the just opened Panama Canal, a few days later they sailed into New York Harbour, arriving on Christmas Eve, some sixty-two days after leaving Newcastle and . . .

And what on earth is this?

Around and about their ship a flotilla has come out to meet them, each craft loaded to the gunwales with a seemingly impossible number of people shouting questions at Les, waving contracts, yelling welcome, taking photographs, the lot.

Forewarned by Tex Rickard that the 'Wonder from Down Under' would be landing, the New York boxing community, managers, media and fans alike, have come out in force to get a first-hand look at him.

As Les would write to Father Coady shortly after arriving, 'It was as funny as a circus, Father. By the time Mr Rickard came aboard there were tugs all around the boat, fight promoters and managers clamouring and scrambling over the ship; fellows with cameras; if there was one man who wanted to be my manager there were one thousand without stretching it a bit.'

Perhaps in an effort to hold off those ravenous hordes of managers — or perhaps because a deal had actually been done, it was never clear — once on the shore Les introduced

Tim O'Sullivan as 'my manager' to the waiting press, and it was assumed thereafter that that was the case. And now, what wasn't as funny as a circus were some of the questions hurled by the press on the shore, as Les became aware for the first time of what he had been accused of at home.

Are you 'a slacker', a 'shirker', a man running away from his 'dooty'?

No, I am not!

What about what the Australian press has been saying about you?

What have they been saying?

And then it started to come out ... Although many of the American press seemed to be in awe of him, treating him as if he was already crowned the world middleweight champion, others had only one subject on their mind and that was 'Why aren't you bearing arms for your country?'

Les gave it to them straight.

'It is all very well for a king to decree that one of his subjects must fight for his country,' he said, 'but when your sovereign asks you to desert your helpless father, your mother, six sisters and five brothers, without leaving them with the necessaries of life, family affection pops up and places a detaining hand upon your shoulder. Some of my compatriots may call me a cur for leaving my country as I did. Probably, many of you Americans will say worse. That is not troubling me in the least. It is my intention to accumulate sufficient funds to enable my parents, sisters and brothers to live. In the war, I would run a 90 per cent chance of being shot fighting for my king. I will take that chance, but not before looking after my family ...

'Please do not give the American public the opinion that I am a deserter. Just inform them that I am one of those individuals who believes that charity begins at home, and that any sacrifice I am to make must be to my family first, and then to my king.'[1]

But time, gentlemen, please. After sorting out the payment of a small fine for the matter of having entered America without a passport, the Australians were free to go.

In short order, Tex whisked Les and O'Sullivan away — both of them goggle-eyed at the sheer size of New York City and the enormous number of people out on the streets — to install them as his guests in New York's luxurious Broztell Hotel on East 27th Street to find their feet.

On the instant Les cabled his mother to tell her that he had arrived safely — and would she call Winnie please? Then it was time for the real press conference downstairs. No matter that Les began the conference by reading a well-prepared statement where he pointed out that all he wanted to do in America was earn some money for his family before enlisting, it was soon clear from the tone of the questions that he was making little headway. The issue of his not doing his 'dooty' for Australia kept rising again and again from the Americans.

In fact, to try to put that whole issue to rest, Les quickly engaged the services of a ghost-writer for the *New York World* newspaper to state his case, and the piece was immediately published. Under the headline, **LES DARCY INSISTS THAT HE IS NOT A SHIRKER**, he poured it out:

'There is nothing of the shirker in my heart.' As a matter of fact he still planned on going to the front, he wrote, and if only the Australian Government had been more co-operative, the whole thing could have been done a lot more easily. Before leaving Australia he had even gone to the military authorities and 'offered [US]$5,000 of my own money as a bond that I would return in six months if they gave me permission to come to America in order to earn enough to keep my mother and father, brothers and sisters in comfort before enlisting.

'You know, some of our boys who went to the trenches are never coming back. I wanted to be sure that my five brothers, four sisters and my mother and father would not want if I was not alive at the end of the war. They are not rich and the brother older than myself is a cripple. Is it unreasonable that I should want to protect them?'

As to his key accuser in Australia, there was another story that bore telling. 'Hugh McIntosh was arranging to take me out of the country. When he thought others were going to do it, he set about preventing my going ... I want to make three or four good fights here, and then O'Sullivan and myself will go to Canada or England and enlist ...'[2]

In any case, Les's chief hope at this point was that all of this malarkey would sort itself out in due course. For the moment at least, such things were mere distractions from the business at hand and that was to get in good physical shape, sustain the *positive* media interest in himself, and then get started on the fighting. Tex Rickard had promised a bout with Georges Carpentier, as soon as he could organise for the gallant Frenchman to get leave from the French Airforce, and come to New York on furlough.

In the meantime, a whirlwind of appearances and things to do beckoned for Les, including making an appearance on stage at the Palace Theatre with 'great escape' artist and illusionist Harry Houdini, where he was introduced to the crowd and received a thunderous round of applause![3] (The irony of appearing with Houdini was not lost on Les, as he wrote a few days later to a friend in Australia, 'The people are good over here. I reckon I am another Houdini ... don't you?'[4])

He also conducted many interviews with journalists hungry for every detail about the 'Australian blacksmith', posed for photographers, engaged in twice-daily training sessions at Billy Grupp's Gymnasium on 116th Street, and had talks with various boxing promoters from other states. Sure, Les could have snapped up one of the offers from the many other promoters, but Tex said that Carpentier was the one, and he was going after nothing less than Madison Square Garden to make all the huge amounts of money work!

A knock on the Broztell Hotel door. Les opens it. It is the young hotel porter, a painfully thin Negro, and he is deeply sorry suh, but there is someone downstairs who is *insisting* on seeing Mistuh Darcy. Sez he is an *Oss*-tralian, too. And he used to be a boxer. The thing is, Mistuh Darcy, it is difficult to know much of him, 'cos he might be drunk, but he sez his name is 'Griff', 'Griffa', sum'n like that?

Young Griffo? The boxing hero of Australia, who had left home shores in 1893 never to return? Great! Show him up!

But Mistuh Darcy, he very drunk, not too good dressed, terrible, rotten, black teeth, and thuh hotel probably wouldn't want likes of him in the building ...

Fine, but please get him!

And so the young porter does, returning shortly afterwards and furtively pushing a fat old drunk man into Mistuh Darcy's room before skedaddling. He is going to catch *hell* from management, if they find out.

And so there they are, Les Darcy and Young Griffo — each a hero before heading to America to seek their international fame and fortune — meeting in a New York hotel room in the early days of 1917. They talk ...

The fact that 'Young Griffo' is no longer young is obvious, as is the fact that the young porter hadn't been exaggerating in his description. Griffo's teeth are *terrible*, he reeks of alcohol, and is evidently doing it very tough indeed. These days one of his tricks to get more alcohol is to take a handkerchief into a bar, stand on it and bet someone that they can't lay a single punch on him for a whole minute while he doesn't take a step off the hankie, but simply dodges and ducks all their blows! No, he couldn't win a real fight in the ring these days, but by God he can still keep himself in grog. They laugh and talk. Les is delighted to meet this Australian legend, and later tips the porter a quarter, telling the disbelieving young man that the 'fat old alko' — as the porter would later describe Griffo, whom he brought up to Les's room — was once one of the greatest featherweight boxers of them all.[5]

★

And while there remained a steady flow of admiring articles about Les in the papers — he was close to the biggest sports story in America at the time — still some columnists wouldn't let up, constantly attacking him for being a shirker. (Are you kidding? A champion boxer running away from his front-line duty, by *stowing away*, all so he can earn money in America? What a great story! And perfect tabloid target.)

From Australia it seemed that Huge Deal McIntosh had used his contacts well, as had Snowy Baker, who continued to send newsletters containing copy with an anti-Darcy slant to American newspapers. Some of it was picked up and reprinted verbatim; some of it was surely reflected in the outpourings of the American sports writers.

The highly influential columnist W.O. McGeehan of the *New York Tribune* made no secret of his own position, and stated firmly that it was 'hard to see how one can make a hero out of Darcy ...'

The highly popular writer Damon Runyon, who had met Snowy Baker when the Australian boxing promoter visited the United States three years earlier and become a close friend, added in his own column that: 'We like to believe that if left to his own devices, Darcy would have joined the colours ... but the commercial eye of the fight promoters recognised his money making possibilities and they caused him to forget his duty ...'

And then, there it was again: **Cold-Footed Les Darcy Bolts From Australia to Escape Home Defense**, reprinted, word for word in the *New York Tribune*, a sure indication of the extraordinary pull that Huge Deal McIntosh had, even in

America's richest city. Tough stuff. Les was a long way from home, missing friends, family, and particularly Winnie, terribly, and most newspapers — both at home, and here in America — seemed to want to attack him. Still, he had one thing going for him, as he wrote in a letter to Maurice O'Sullivan late at night on the first day of January.

> There is a power of money in the game here, Maurice. Just imagine if I was getting 30,000 dollars to box a man 10 rounds. The mistake I made is not coming over here 12 months ago ... Never mind, I have my best years before me ... I have one ambition and that is to get rich and get rich quick.[6]

As to the newspaper attacks, Les had just one thing to say about that:

> They made some squeal. But why should I worry and get a red nose? I've seen a few papers over here and they certainly did roast me. They couldn't say anything worse. Now they talk about seizing my property. If they do, I'll get some more, that's all. I have still got my lovely life and limbs and no holes through me.[7]

To another friend, shortly afterwards, Les confessed he was having some troubles with the bloke he had come over with, 'Sully', but had another solution there, too.

> I have sent for old Mick. At least he is honest ...[8]

Up in East Maitland, Mary Newton received a letter of her own. Inside was a simple form headed **EFFECTS OF DECEASED OFFICERS OR OTHER RANKS**, and it informed her that Package 6624 had arrived from overseas, containing the final personal effects of her son, Private Eric Newton, No. 147, of the Australian 1st Light Horse: *letters, tin, postcards, hair brush, pair of gloves, two comforters and an armlet.*[9]

The days passed and still there was no hoped-for word from Tex to the effect that Carpentier had been lined up. So Les made a decision. To earn some money while waiting, Les would go on a 'vaudeville tour' of America's mid-west with Freeman Bernstein's Burlesque Show, doing exhibitions with a friendly American boxer by the name of Freddie Gilmore. It was a measure of just how strong a drawcard Les was thought to be in America that his initial contract guaranteed him US$2,500 a *week*, for fifteen weeks.

Nevertheless, the American press took, generally, a very dim view of it, with the principal newspaper of Connecticut leading the way when the subject was mooted: 'Les Darcy is not going to fight just yet. The call of drama is luring him as insistently as the call that brought him fifteen thousand miles or so away from Australia where the simple-minded people of the Bush seem to feel that a fighter's place is in the trenches at this particular time. Les has decided that the call of drama must be answered. He feels for the stage in this vicinity. The ears that were deaf to the uncouth suggestion of the recruiting sergeant in Sydney, Australia, are quick to the pleas of high minded theatrical agents rustling greenbacks as they demand that Darcy come forth and elevate the drama.'[10]

Actually, Les and his chosen promoter had a drama all their own when the first stop of the tour, in New Jersey, suddenly had to be cancelled. Apparently some obscure state law made it illegal for a boxer to appear in a stage show and, for some reason, the state authorities suddenly decided to enforce it.[11]

And so it went. Another night, another town. Moving on, moving on, all the time moving on. In some places the crowds were better than others, but mostly the whole thing was a fairly wretched experience, compounded by Les receiving a telegram from Tex informing him that not only was the Carpentier fight proving impossible to organise — the French authorities simply weren't interested in letting him go, and it wasn't even certain that Carpentier wanted to come — but he had lost the bid to lease Madison Square Garden for a year, and ... in short ... Les was on his own.

Good luck.

For the moment there was little Les could do but continue on the vaudeville tour and wait to see what other offers came up.

One thing that lifted his spirits a great deal was when Mick Hawkins at last caught up with him in Pittsburgh at the end of January — having left Australia, at Margaret Darcy's behest, by ship in early December, even before Les had sent for him. Relatively anonymous, he had had no trouble in getting a passport. The two men warmly shook hands and took a good look at each other. Good ol' Mick didn't look a day different. He never did. He was just Mick. A bloke with a face like a twisted sandshoe, who was as honest as the day was long and was as faithful a friend as Les ever had ...

Mick, however, didn't like what he saw at all. Les looked 'butcher's hook' *crook*. Whereas he had always been so bursting with energy and strength, he seemed now rather skinny, pale and shivering. He had a cough that didn't seem to go away.

Are you all right, Les?

Of course he was right, Les replied. The doctors had told him his cough and his feeling slightly out of sorts was probably because he was not used to an American winter, and that once the snows melted and the spring came, so too would he soon be feeling as right as rain again.

But forget all that, Mick! The letters! Do you have letters for me?

Mick certainly did, most especially letters from Winnie, which Les happily devoured. Goodness but he missed her. And, as was clear from her letters, she missed him terribly. On the spot, Les did what he did most days, which was to write Winnie another letter. Some days, back in Australia, Winnie would receive as many as five letters at a time.

As it happened, with Mick now with him again, Les felt things would soon turn around. A particular problem that he had at this stage was endless confusion regarding who precisely was managing him. For the last month since arriving in New York his relationship with Tim O'Sullivan had become extremely strained, the more so because the older man was claiming that Les had a signed contract making him, Sully, the manager on an outrageous *third* of his earnings. True, O'Sullivan didn't have a copy of that contract, but that was only because, he claimed, it had disappeared from his bag while they were on the *Hattie Luckenbach* — the clear implication being that Les had stolen it. The situation came to a head when Les returned from the vaudeville tour to find it announced in the papers that O'Sullivan had lined him up for a bout with the famous Mike Gibbons in Milwaukee, a bout that Les knew nothing about.

To try to clarify the business, and make it clear that he was handling his own affairs, Les even penned a letter to the American press, which was published. The letter concluded, 'I beg to notify that I have no contract whatever to box Mike Gibbons on April 10 or at any other time ... No one has authority to sign articles for me without my approval. Mr. E.T. O'Sullivan is no longer in my employ, either as trainer or otherwise, having been dismissed Tuesday Feb. 13.'[12]

Never mind. The demand for Les's services was still high and, after some to-ing and fro-ing, the man who now had the lease on Madison Square Garden, the millionaire Grant Hugh Browne, had in short order locked Les in for a long-awaited fight there with Jack Dillon on 5 March 1917 on a guaranteed purse of US$30,000.

Thirty *thousand* dollars. The equivalent of £6,000 back home! Les and Mick quickly moved out to Browne's property, Brownleigh Park at Goshen, about forty miles north of New York City, and began full-on training. Mr Brown gave the two Australians enormous red dressing-gowns to put on between training sessions — Les soon sheepishly dubbed his a 'flamin' kimono'[13] — and they were away!

It was looking as if things were going to go well for Les in America, after a fairly tumultuous start.

When it came to having a bee in her bonnet, few made a more impressive, or pretty, figure than Lily Molloy. And this bee was buzzing, because Lily had decided that she was going to America to seek her fame and fortune in Hollywood and she wanted her best friend, Winnie O'Sullivan, to accompany her. To begin with it would be a wonderful adventure, and it might also help Winnie shake off some of that melancholy that had been with her since the terrible day that Eileen died. Plus, of course, Les was over there, so it all made sense!

Winnie's parents, Sarah and Patrick O'Sullivan, did not think so at all. It was out of the question. *Out of the question.* Winnie was too young to make such a trip, and certainly too young to be in America, unchaperoned, with Les. This was no reflection on their enormous affection for Les Darcy, just a reality. It was only a certain type of woman who would travel, unmarried, with a man, and their daughter was not that type of woman. She was a lady. They were sorry, but the answer was *no*.

Oh no, it wasn't.

Thoroughly modern Lily Molloy was simply not a woman to take no for an answer, and she came up with something of a solution. Her reckoning was that if her highly respectable brother, Jack — who also had Hollywood ambitions — and her aunt, the very proper, very stout, very stoical Miss Mary Dwyer, accompanied them, and promised never to leave Winnie's side, it would *have* to be all right. Without further ado she arranged to visit Winnie and her parents at the Lord Dudley, with Jack and her auntie in tow.

There were tears, there was tea. There were promises, exhortations and hand-wringing. But in the end it was done. Under the conditions that Lily laid out — and chiefly because the O'Sullivans were impressed by the very no-nonsense Miss Dwyer — they agreed to the proposal. Winnie was going to the United States of America. And she was allowed to see Les![14]

And then the heaviest blow of all fell.

On 2 March 1917, just three days before the fight was due to take place — at a time when his announcement could be expected to garner maximum publicity — the most powerful political figure in New York, Governor Charles S. Whitman, announced that the fight between Les Darcy and Jack Dillon was *off* because he was personally banning the Australian from taking part in any boxing match in New York.

And for good reason, dammit.

For, as the Governor told the *New York Times*: '... Darcy, so I am informed, is a runaway from his own country. In disguise and under an alias, he left his native land because he was afraid to fight in the cause for which his fellow-countrymen are sacrificing their lives. He prefers to give a brutal exhibition at some personal risk for a purse of $30,000. I believe that the citizens of this State will support the Governor in his insistence that this thing shall not be permitted in New York.'[15]

Both Les Darcy and Mick Hawkins were, naturally

enough, devastated by the Governor's decision. *This* was happening in the land of the free and the home of the brave? For his part, Grant Hugh Browne was both stupefied and outraged. Les Darcy might have broken a relatively minor Australian law in departing without permission or a passport, but he had broken *no* American law since he'd been in the country, and had entered into a lawful contract to fight a reputable American boxer. Far from supporting the Governor in his insistence that this thing not be permitted in New York, there were at least 20,000 New Yorkers who were prepared to part with big money for a ticket to see it happen! And why on earth was Les being singled out as the poster boy for 'shirkers', just as he had been in Australia? After all, England had conscription, and yet there were plenty of British actors and boxers plying their trades in America with never a single voice raised against them!

None of *them,* however, garnered remotely the attention that a man as famous as Darcy did, and for that fame alone it was his fate to be buffeted by the political currents of the day. 'Has it ever occurred to you,' Les said to one New York journalist, 'that I am the first man who has ever come to the United States and was not permitted to make a living? Of course, I realise that mine is a most unusual case. All that publicity that has been given me, which generally is so desirable, reacted against me. I am prevented from pursuing my occupation while alien opera-singers, waiters, bootblacks and whatnot are allowed to make their livelihood.

'I am not a "slacker". The term is even more obnoxious to me than it is to you folks on this side because you have not realised the real significance of it. I am not running away from my duty. I am doing my duty as I see it. I have eleven people dependent on me. I am the second oldest of ten children. My father is sixty years old, crippled from rheumatism, and unable to work. I have one brother older than me. He is twenty-two, but also a cripple. I am twenty-one. Then comes Frank, seventeen, Pearl sixteen, Jack fourteen, Ted, twelve, Muriel eleven, Lily nine, Kitty eight and baby Joe. He is about eighteen months old now, and in the last letter I had from home my mother tells me he was just beginning to toddle around and talk. Gee, I would like to see him.'[16]

For the moment the only way forward seemed to be to try to change the Governor's mind, and when Les happened to see the man himself in the foyer of the St Regis Hotel on the night of 6 March, he decided to grasp the opportunity. Rushing up to him, he introduced himself and asked if he could have a few words? He was very keen to explain, to prove, that he was not a slacker, that he had offered to enlist in Australia but was under age and that there were solid reasons why he had done what he had done. In response, Governor Whitman told him that this was neither the time nor the place, but he would be happy to receive him and talk about it in a couple of days' time.[17]

Done.

The promised meeting with Governor Whitman took place at his official Queen Anne residence in Albany, in upstate New York, a few days later. The Governor listened carefully as Grant Hugh Browne and Les stated their case, plainly, simply — with Mick Hawkins there, too, as ever, as Les's backup.

Browne's case was that the Governor had no *right* to do what he had done. Les's only misdemeanour was to have entered the country without a passport, for which he had already paid a small fine, and apart from that he was a lawful person, pursuing his lawful profession.

As to Les, he tried to explain to the Governor that all he wanted was a *chance*, a chance to earn some money for his family, and then he would join up . . .

And the Governor made his own case in reply. His words would ring in Mick Hawkins's ears for decades to come: 'I haven't got anything against you, Darcy . . . but there's a guy named McIntosh who must have a big pull back in Australia. I just can't allow you to fight.'[18] And so he didn't.

There was nothing for it but to pack up, move on and seek fights in other states. In all the commentary that followed, it was a columnist for the *New York World* who was perhaps most astute, observing on 11 March: 'In all the history of the ring there has never been a man in Darcy's predicament. One of the greatest boxers that ever visited America, and surely the greatest drawing card, he is compelled to pick up his traps and leave the very centre of fistiana to try his luck in other states. Should Governor Whitman's official disapproval spread beyond New York, then indeed will Darcy begin to wish that he had never stowed away out of Australia to avoid military duty.'

★

In Australia, in certain circles, the news of what had happened to the stowaway was greeted with glee. In Sydney, the Reverend C.H. Talbot exulted, to the applause of his Presbyterian Assembly, that 'the champion prize-fighter of Australia shirked his duty to King and country and sneaked away to America. But they've got him now!'[19]

It was not an easy letter for Les to write, but in the end he felt he simply had to do it. He was homesick, he had been in America for nearly three months and still hadn't fought, he missed Winnie terribly, he had been attacked by the media on two continents. Could it be that the solution to at least some of his problems was to head home?

15th March

Dear Mr Baker,

You will no doubt be anxious to know of my whereabouts and doings, despite the mean way in which I left you. I am very sorry indeed to have left the way I did, but I thought I was doing the best.

I thought if I told you I was going you would have me stopped for sure. I tried to do the right thing. I offered the authorities £1000 before I left to let me come over here for six months, and then go home and enlist, but they turned me down.

To tell you the truth, Mr Baker, I did not want to go to the war just then, and I don't think anybody else in my position would want to go, either. I have, as you know, right now I have a chance of setting my family on *their feet for the rest of their lives, and can do it in a short time: then I don't care what becomes of me.*

I'll go to the front, but I think I would be a bigger cur if I went to the front and left a starving family at home. The British Army wouldn't miss me for a few months ...

If the authorities over in Australia will overlook my wrongdoings, I will return and enlist in the Australian Army.

Snowy Baker had no sooner read the letter than he arranged to have it published, in full, in Huge Deal McIntosh's sporting publication the *Referee*. Vindication! The mighty Les Darcy, practically *begging* to come home. (The prospect must have been a good one for Baker, however. Back in Sydney, the boxing game had fallen on hard times indeed, with paltry fighters stoushing before small crowds, and a general air of decay hanging over the whole thing.)

The one saving grace for Les Darcy after the fight in New York fell through was that there were still offers for bouts in other states. In short order — have gloves, will travel — he and Mick Hawkins were on their way, going out after them. As they did so, Les kept writing home to everyone. Almost always, these postcards were upbeat, maintaining that despite the negative press, he was getting on all right. Typical, was a card he wrote to a friend by the name of Thomas Molony, care of the Lord Dudley Hotel in Paddington.

Dear Tom,

Just a card to say hello.

They have stopped me boxing here but I expect to get going soon. I am keeping well and having a royal time, so can't complain. We have seen quite a lot of the country down south ...

Kind regards to all the boys at home ...

Les

In fact, however, in private Les was far from happy. What didn't help, apart from everything else, was that he never quite felt well, never quite had the energy that he'd had in Australia, and still couldn't shake off a persistent cough that he'd had since arriving in New York. Certainly, he came across as happy enough in public, but still, sometimes astute journalists who interviewed him could extract from him sentiments that were a lot less upbeat than the ones he was sending home in postcards.

One of those journalists wrote in his paper in Philadelphia: 'Les Darcy, the marvellous Australian champion, is a fatalist. He believes his end is not far off. He is prepared to die ...'

The journalist quoted, once again, Les's justifications as to why he had come to America, with the difference being that this time Les highlighted how much more important those reasons were than simply joining up at home.

'My people come first with me, even before my country,' Les said. 'I don't believe I'll survive the war. I expect it and I'm ready for it. I'm ready to do my duty but I would be shirking a duty if I gave my life before I provided for my own. So while I'm here I'll fight anybody they offer bar none, the devil himself if need be, to get money . . .'[20]

George Chip certainly wasn't the devil, but as soon as a promoter in Ohio promised a Chip versus Darcy rematch on attractive terms, Les and Mick were on their way to the heart of the American Midwest . . .

And yet Les and Mick had no sooner arrived than the same thing happened as before! Governor James M. Cox's move to follow Governor Whitman's lead by banning Les from boxing struck the blow, and the editorial in the *Cleveland Press,* on 31 March 1917, provided the sting. Headlined **DON'T CHANGE YOUR MIND DARCY** the editors didn't miss their mark, with the final two paragraphs being particularly sharp.

> '"Slacker,"' the crowd called him. "Undesirable," Governor Whitman called him. And bade him begone.
> 'That's the way Ohio and Cleveland feel about it too.
> 'ON YOUR WAY, DARCY.'[21]

A pariah indeed. The one thing that gave Les heart at this point was that while government institutions and the media were against him, he still seemed to receive a warm welcome from the people themselves — and with his ability to make friends easily he at least kept his spirits up enough to keep going.

★

It was April Fools' Day but this was no joke. When the message reached the editor of the *New York World,* Frank Cobb, that the President of the United States, Woodrow Wilson, wanted to see him urgently, he was instantly on his way to the White House from his Washington hotel room. No matter that it was rising midnight, he felt sure the President would still be up. Sure enough, when Cobb arrived a short time later, he was ushered into his presence. Cobb — a long-time confidant of the President — had never seen him look worse. Haggard and harried, Woodrow Wilson obviously hadn't slept in nights and the reason was soon spelt out.

In grave tones, the President told Cobb that he was likely to go before Congress the next day and ask that America declare war on Germany. 'I think I know what war means,' he continued. 'It would mean that we should lose our heads along with the rest and stop weighing right and wrong. It would mean that a majority of people in this hemisphere would go war-mad, quit thinking, and devote their energies to destruction . . .'

'It means an attempt to reconstruct a peacetime civilization with war standards, and at the end of the war there will be no bystanders with sufficient power to influence the terms. There won't be any peace standards left to work with. There will be only war standards.'[22]

What he wanted to do now, he said, was go over his reasoning with Cobb and see if there was *any* way out, any alternative that might present itself rather than *cry havoc and let slip the dogs of war!*

There was no doubt in Wilson's mind that Germany had been a terrible aggressor, that America's interests had been severely damaged — the sinking of the *Lusitania* had been a bare beginning — and, most crucially, that the weight of American arms and industry would indeed be able to stop them. But again, was there *any* way out, short of war, that Cobb could see?

'What else can I do?' he asked the editor. 'Is there anything else I can do? If there is any alternative, for God's sake, let's take it . . .'

Cobb told him, regretfully, that no, there really wasn't anything else he could do other than declare war; that there was no alternative. His hand had been forced by Germany, and there was no way America could remain above the fray.

Still Wilson kept worrying about it, even later into the night . . . 'Once lead this people into war,' the American President said, 'and they'll forget there ever was such a thing as tolerance. To fight you must be brutal and ruthless, and the spirit of ruthless brutality will enter into the very fiber of our national life, infecting Congress, the courts, the policeman on the beat, the man in the street.

'Conformity will be the only virtue, and every man who refuses to conform will have to pay the penalty.'[23]

Cobb left him in the early hours of morning, convinced that the American President was set for war.

Les Darcy was passing through Chicago when the news broke. Extra! Extra! Read all about it! Emblazoned across the top of the *Chicago Daily Tribune* on the morning of 3 April 1917, it read in enormous black type:

U.S. AT WAR: WILSON.
'WE MUST FIGHT FOR JUSTICE AND RIGHTS.'
President Tells Joint Session of Congress
That German Monarchy
Is Threat To All Mankind

Much the same war fever that had gripped Australia began to grip America. Flags waved freely. The *Star Spangled Banner* was heard everywhere. Every headline, every radio bulletin, and every utterance pointed to the war, just as every road and railway track seemed to lead to an army camp where fresh recruits could be turned into soldiers.

Just wait till 'Our boys get among them!'

Could Les stand against this tide any longer? He could not. After consultations with the ever faithful Mick, he decided to take fairly radical action and swim with the tide.

All but on the spot Darcy took the Oath of Allegiance at the Circuit Court of Cook County, Illinois, and signified his intention of becoming an American. Les's comments were widely reported in the newspapers: 'I like the United States, although I can't say that the United States has shown any great liking for me . . . and at the earliest opportunity it is my intention to become a naturalized citizen.'[24]

Maybe, see, if he was not viewed as a total outsider in America his worst attackers would call off the dogs. And the folks back home, following his every move via his letters and the constant newspaper reports of his movements? He felt that they — and Winnie, who was even then en route to him — would understand. And he was right. They took it for what it was, not an abandonment of Australia but a necessary technical manoeuvre to be able to keep going, to achieve his dream of earning enough money to be able to set the family up.

With that settled, Les set off in the company of Mick Hawkins and training partner Freddie Gilmore, with whom he had become friendly on the vaudeville tour. They were on their way to New Orleans, Louisiana, to fight the opponent who had caused Les the most controversy in his career to date — Jeff Smith. Everything was set this time, and nothing could go wrong. Les had a great training camp an hour away from where the fight would take place, on the Gulf of Mexico; Smith was so keen for the bout that he could hardly raise spit; and Les had been assured and reassured that the political situation was now benign. Sweet as . . .

A nut.

The Governor of Louisiana had to be a nut! Just a week before the fight was due to take place, Governor Ruffin Golson Pleasant fell in with all the rest and barred Les from fighting in his state. The Governor's cable, sent on 13 April 1917 to the manager of the Louisiana Auditorium read: 'Please cancel boxing match between Darcy and Smith. Make this request for public good. Let Darcy follow noble example of Georges Carpentier before seeking athletic engagements in Louisiana.'[25]

Appalled to his core, Les had few doubts now that he was the victim of an orchestrated campaign, which went right to the top. As he wrote in a long letter to Maurice O'Sullivan:

The Governor here is alright but Whitman got the Heads at Washington and got them to stop it the dirty dog.[26]

Les had had just about enough and even went so far as to nominate the ship he would like to return home on — the *Sonoma,* leaving on 5 June from San Francisco. And then, seemingly out of a clear blue sky, a 39-year-old flamboyant boxing promoter from Memphis by the name of Billy Haack Senior decided to take a chance on the Australian. For, this kindly man with a twist — all cigar smoke, bluster and genuine southern charm — now came to visit Les at his Louisiana training camp and told him he had an idea about how to break the whole log jam. Haack, see, was close to the Mayor of Memphis and reckoned they could do a deal with him. Would Les come on down to Memphis to see him?

Les would. With Mick and Freddie Gilmore in tow, he was soon on the train to Tennessee, soaking up the sight of the mighty Mississippi — and wondering what awaited him this time ...

Memphis proved to have an extraordinarily large black population, more Negroes than Les had ever seen in his life, but it was white men who ran it, and, only shortly after arriving, Billy Haack Senior had him in the office of Mayor Thomas Ashcroft.

Now, for the first time since he had landed in America, Les

had the chance to state his whole case to a public official who was prepared to give him a full hearing, without fear or favour.

'I've seen too many men come back from the trenches, unfit to earn a living for the rest of their lives,' he told the Mayor. 'All I ask is that I am allowed to fight for my family before I go to the trenches. If I can play them in a position where they will want for nothing when I am gone, I will be satisfied.'[27]

Ashcroft promptly agreed that Les had been hardly done by, most particularly by the damned northern Yankees, led by that wretch Whitman and he proposed a deal. Les agreed to the terms and the Mayor immediately dispatched a telegram to both Tennessee's powerful representative in Washington, Senator K.D. McKella, and to the Secretary of War, Mr Newton D. Baker. It read:

Les Darcy, Australian champion boxer, is a volunteer for service in the American Army. He offers his services through the Mayor of Memphis if you will agree to give him leave of absence during June and July to fill boxing dates. Darcy as volunteer would mean great recruiting boom in every city he visits. He is anxious to do the best thing possible and I ask you to accept his offer. Please return wire this afternoon.

T.C. Ashcroft, Mayor.[28]

Les and Mick were back at Memphis's very fine Peabody Hotel that evening with another Australian boxer by the name of Mick King when they got the word. The deal was accepted. It was on! Les was so excited he did something of a jig around the room with Mick King. At last, at last, things were going to sort themselves out.

On 20 April 1917 Les Darcy released a formal announcement to the newspapers. He would, he said, 'enlist under the American colours' so long as he was granted leave by the military authorities to fulfil commitments he had for several fights in June and July.[29]

On 24 April 1917 it happened. Sergeant James Leslie Darcy, of the US Signal Corps Aviation Section, reporting for duty, *suh!* At ease, sergeant, and report back here in two months' time. (In fact, as Les knew, he never would have to report back because a further condition he had put on his enlistment was that, once joined up, he would be immediately transferred to 'an Australian Army'.[30])

Did the tide start to turn Les's way again? It would seem so. As the *New York World* immediately observed, 'No more can he be called a slacker',[31] and there seemed to be little argument. For on 25 April two years to the day since the Anzacs had landed at Gallipoli, Governor Whitman's reaction to the news of Darcy's enlistment was also positive and reported in the newspapers.

'I am gratified that Les Darcy has enlisted,' the Governor said, 'and I sincerely hope that others of the profession will follow his example as I am quite sure their services can be of the greatest value in our hour of need.'[32]

Surely now all the other governors would fall in line with him, just as they had last time ...

A phone call! It was Winnie on the line. Both she and Les had to SHOUT down the scratchy line to make themselves heard, but that was no trouble. Winnie had landed safely in LOS ANGELES, after a rather nervous dash from Hawaii across the Pacific, fearing German submarines all the way. Miss Dwyer had insisted we wear LIFE JACKETS all the way across. Les had organised his next fight in Memphis and everything was going to be all right! LILY is going to her first screen auditions tomorrow, and is so excited! And we met CHARLIE CHAPLIN and his wife in Hawaii, and we're staying at a flat in downtown Los Angeles! And you, Les, how are you? Yes, his throat had been a little sore lately, and he still hadn't quite shaken off the cough, but everything should come GOOD, just as it was with his boxing! Should she come to him IMMEDIATELY? No, Win, ENJOY LOS ANGELES! Have a lovely holiday. I have taken the OATH of ALLEGIANCE! Let me get this fight in MEMPHIS done, and *THEN* come, Win! Everything is going to BE ALL RIGHT![33]

Now with what seemed like a new lease of life, Les prepared for the fight against an accomplished boxer from Milwaukee by the name of Len Rowlands with renewed vigour. *Now* he was going to show 'em! *Now* all the agonies of the previous months could be quickly forgotten. And now, by the time dear Winnie caught up with him, he'd be rolling in it!

Now ... now ... actually, now he suddenly felt very weak.

In late April as Les was coming down the steps of Memphis City Hall in the company of Freddie Gilmore and Mick Hawkins, Mick suddenly became aware that he and Freddie were walking on their own. He casually looked back, and there was Les, hanging on to the railing for dear life. 'My legs have gone on me,' he explained. From parts unknown, a sudden wave of weakness had broken over the mighty boxer with such force on those steps that he simply couldn't stand up.[34]

As rough a man as Mick Hawkins was, when it came to the care of Les he could be as gentle and nurturing as a mother with a newborn baby, and he now slowly eased Les to a sitting position on the steps to get his breath, while Freddie went for help. In short order they got Les to St Joseph's Hospital in New Orleans, where the doctor opened Les's mouth to take a look and was immediately reaching for the forceps to remove a badly abscessed tooth — one of the same ones that Harold Hardwick had snapped off fifteen months previously. Still, however, with no immediate improvement in his condition, Les was moved to the nearby Gartley Ramsey Private Hospital where his unmistakably infected tonsils were also removed.

To Mick, things didn't look too flash, but then came the good news — the doctors told him that despite how weak Les was now, his recovery would be rapid and he should be back to his old self and ready to fight in a week or so. Mick's shoulders sagged with relief, and he immediately made arrangements with the promoter to get the fight postponed by just a bit.

At Les's insistence, Mick wrote to Winnie in Los Angeles to say that Les had been operated on for tonsillitis but everything was fine. She should continue to enjoy her holiday. He would recover, have the fight and *then* she could come.

A few days later, though, it was obvious that Les wasn't recovering as expected. He continued to lose weight, sleep poorly and drift in and out of a fierce fever. Now even getting out of his hospital bed was impossible. To Mick's eyes he was wasting away. The days turned into a week, and then a fortnight. The fight with Len Rowlands was cancelled.

In Les's lucid moments he never complained of the tremendous pain and discomfort he obviously felt, and the nurses and doctors marvelled at his courage — but after three weeks had passed since he'd fallen ill, those moments were short and his hours of unconsciousness getting longer. Sometimes, it seemed that he had fallen into a near coma. Still, on one occasion Les came out of his stupor just long enough to say, 'The count is seven, Jack Dillon, but they'll never count ten over me.'[35]

On another occasion, when Les awoke, Mick was able to talk to him. 'How going, Friday?' he asked, using his nickname for Les.

'Not so good, Old Horse ...' Les replied grimly, faintly, before sighing softly and slipping back into the depths whence he came.[36]

At this point the good sister who was in the room and had been holding Les's hand, put it back on Les's chest, brought up the other hand to join it and placed a crucifix between them. 'Go now, and pray for him a while,' she gently told Mick. 'There is nothing more.'[37]

It was obvious now that a certain point had been reached — maybe even that of no return — and Mick cabled Winnie in California ...

It was a Saturday night, and Winnie and Lily had just returned from confession at a downtown Los Angeles church to find Miss Dwyer and Jack Molloy in a highly agitated state. A telegram had arrived for her, they explained, and the news wasn't good. It was from Mick Hawkins and it said:

Les sinking fast in private hospital in Memphis.
Please come at once.[38]

A series of urgent phone calls ensued to ascertain precisely where Les was, and by the following day Winnie — who was shocked to her core — and Miss Dwyer were on their way east. They arrived at the railway station in Memphis late on the evening of 23 May 1917. Winnie was desperate to get to Les as quickly as possible, while also fearful about what she would see when she found him. She still couldn't quite believe that it was as bad as Mick had said it was. '*Sinking fast*'? Surely not her Les, always so full of love, laughter and *life* ... And yet, so too had her sister Eileen been just like that, before she had died. Please, please, *dear* God, spare poor Les ...

Alas, from the first moments of arriving, there was malevolence in this Memphis air, a deep foreboding, as their cab made its way through the city streets to Les's hospital.

Stop! The taxi-driver came to an abrupt halt, the way blocked by a large group of men shouting in the street and kicking something around, something that the headlights showed to be an oddly contoured soccer ball or the like. Peering into the semi-darkness, the driver gave a sudden start, threw the cab in reverse and tore off down a side street. As it turned out, what they had thought was a 'soccer ball' in the shadows of the night was actually the charred head of a black man who had been lynched the day before they arrived. Though there had not been a skerrick of proof, it had been thought likely the deaf and dumb unfortunate had been responsible for the recent murder of a young white girl, and so they had hanged him on suspicion.[39] Winnie and her chaperone had stumbled into the grisly aftermath of one of the last such barbaric acts in the tortured history of the American South ...

Evil was in the air.

At Winnie's first sight of Les in the hospital she knew that her love was in serious trouble. With all his weakness and wasting away, one of the most feared fighters in all the world now looked like a very young boy again. He still had the strength, though, to say: 'Oh Winnie, when they told me you were here, I thought they were joking me.'[40]

Miss Dwyer, Mick Hawkins and Freddie Gilmore quietly left the room so the two could be alone to softly talk. And really, Les did seem to perk up a bit in Winnie's presence. After getting updates on what everyone at home had been doing when she'd left, and what she'd heard since, Les asked Winnie to be sure to write to his mother to tell her that he was going to be all right.

'Mum thinks I am going to die,' he weakly laughed, 'but I'm not ...'[41]

Late that night Winnie reluctantly left Les at the nurse's insistence that the patient must rest, and she and Miss Dwyer were found lodgings for the evening. When Winnie returned the following morning, exhausted after a restless night, she was greeted with the news that her man was poorly and that she mustn't stay long because it would be too tiring for him.

As Winnie came into the room, Mick, Fred, the promoter Billy Haack Senior and a nurse all moved away from the bed so she could see him. Les looked up, smiled wanly, a mere echo of the smile he had once beamed, spoke to her briefly, and said he felt sleepy. He was drifting ... just drifting ... drifting ... away ...

Winnie — torn between the desire to stay, go, weep, remain strong, *howl* like she had when she had seen Eileen with precisely the same kind of weakness — whispered a little into Les's ear, stroked his brow, said her goodbyes, and turned to go, as her love softly closed his eyes. The young Australian woman had just reached the door, when the nurse called her back: 'Come quickly!'

Winnie ran back to the bed and instinctively knew what had happened — as much as she tried to fight the realisation — even before she threw her arms around him.

Les was gone. It was 1.45 pm, on the 24th of May, 1917.

If, as they say, the human spirit moves upwards from the moment of death and looks down upon its earthly body left behind, Les would have seen Winnie embracing him, refusing to believe he had left her, tears and anguish all around. While the convulsively crying Winnie was held tightly by Miss Dwyer, Mick refused all attempts to be comforted, and simply sat there beside the bed sobbing uncontrollably, as he held Les's hand and rocked back and forth, buffeted by ever more waves of misery.[42]

So, too, the nurses and doctors, who seemed to appear from everywhere and also began to cry. Being professionally dispassionate might have been their ideal, but over the previous three weeks they had all come to admire the spirit of this Australian man so much that his death was a bitter, bitter blow.[43]

The headline of the *Memphis Press* on the following day set the tone for much of the coverage that followed: **LES DARCY DIES OF BROKEN HEART. MAN WITHOUT A COUNTRY.** The official death certificate, though, is more prosaic. According to the doctors of the Gartley Ramsey Hospital who examined him, Les Darcy died of 'streptococcus septicaemia, septic endocarditis and lobar pneumonia'.[44] What it boiled down to was that the two teeth knocked out by Hardwick and which had so hastily been put back in had turned septic and deadly. The resulting infection had, bit by bit, spread through his body, finally overwhelming his immune system and killing him as surely as a bullet to the heart.

A touching thing occurred in the twenty-four hours immediately after Les's death, as the news spread. The sporting community across America seemed to rise up en masse, in support of one of their own, and Mick Hawkins was inundated with offers from sporting bodies to pick up the expenses of either having a funeral and burial in Memphis or sending the body home.

The worst thing Mick had to do was cable Les's mother with the news, and her curt telegram of reply was quick:

Send Body Home. Expenses paid at this end.
Darcy.[45]

The bereaved Margaret Darcy's wishes for her Les to come home were of course respected, but the Memphis Phoenix Club, the largest sporting club in the Tennessee capital, insisted on meeting all expenses, including the cost of having Les's body embalmed and placed in a beautiful vacuum-sealed aluminium casket with glass top, which fitted into a larger wooden casing — the whole thing looking like an enormous and elaborate jewellery box.

The first of what would be no fewer than four funerals for Les Darcy was held in St Brigid's Church, Memphis, with Les's coffin draped in both the American and the Australian flags and the church 'packed to the rafters' with representatives of the sports community of Tennessee and America's east, in much the same manner as his fights back in Rushcutters Bay used to be.

From there, with Winnie weeping beside — clutching a single lock of his hair which she had snipped from him on the day that he died[46] — Les's coffin was escorted by members of America's National Guard, the Catholic Boy

Scouts, the Chickasaw baseball team (whom he'd travelled with on the train to Memphis), slow-marching to the railway station as a military band played:

Nearer, my God, to Thee, nearer to Thee!
E'en though it be a cross that raiseth me,
Still all my song shall be, nearer, my God, to Thee;
Nearer, my God, to Thee,
Nearer to Thee!
Though like the wanderer, the sun gone down,
Darkness be over me, my rest a stone;
Yet in my dreams I'd be nearer, my God, to Thee; nearer, my
    God, to Thee, nearer to Thee! . . .
There let the way appear, steps unto heaven;
All that Thou sendest me, in mercy given;
Angels to beckon me nearer, my God, to Thee;
Nearer, my God, to Thee, nearer to Thee!

Les's casket-encased body, in the company of the still completely shattered Mick Hawkins and Winnie O'Sullivan, then began a journey across the American continent, with the train saluted and cried over along the way by people who came out in the night merely to see it pass, to kneel on the platform and pray for his soul.

Les had never set foot in San Francisco in his life, but in death the city turned on what would be described as 'the grandest funeral ever given a foreign sportsman', organised by the sports community in that fair city. Even before the service began, Mick was presented with a silver plate, upon which was engraved crossed American and Australian flags, above a dedication:

Les Darcy.
In Memoriam, from his friends and admirers in San Francisco, 1917.[47]

Inside the Eagles Hall auditorium, where the service was held, the Reverend Father Joseph J. McQuaide reached for the heights in his oration: 'We are engaged in the transportation homeward of all that is mortal of one, a mere boy in years, whom we knew only by reputation; of one who in life had not put his foot in this City of the Golden Gate; yet we bear gently, as our hearts, touched by the pathos of this boy's sad ending impels us, these, his remains, to the good ship that will carry them over the trackless Pacific Ocean, to have them finally rest at home, touched by the hands and moistened by the tears of a heartbroken mother ...'[48]

From the church to the wharf this time, the coffin was once again draped in the American and Australian flags and escorted through streets thick with mourners, led by a thousand of San Francisco's finest sports people. They had all come out to pay their respects to a man they never knew, but who was one of theirs all the same. A sportsman, pure and simple ...

On 5 June, they loaded Les's coffin onto the SS *Sonoma* with care, their bared heads bowed, holding their hats to their chests, as the band played 'Auld Lang Syne'. This was pathos pure, as it was the very same boat Les had said he might return on in a letter to a friend back home two months earlier.

Winnie would travel above, often quietly weeping in a deckchair — with Mick Hawkins powerless to comfort her — while Les lay, cold, in the hold below.

On the misty morning of Tuesday 26 June 1917 — a dark, cold day — the *Sonoma* sailed through the heads of Sydney Harbour, bringing the body of Les Darcy back to the land of his birth, some nine months after he had left it, and just over a month since he had died. Sydney was waiting for him, with so many trying to get onto the docks at Walsh Bay that only the select few with passes were allowed through the gates of the compound. An ashen-faced Ned Darcy was there with his elder children, Cecil, Frosty, Pearlie and Jack, all waiting to receive the body of their son and brother, flesh of their flesh, blood of their blood, spirit of their spirit — and they were joined by some of their most faithful friends from East Maitland. Too, the O'Sullivan family had turned out in force, not only to provide moral support to the Darcys but also to clasp their nineteen-year-old Winnie back to their bosom as soon as they could.

The rest of the people, a huge and heaving mass, had to watch through the wrought-iron gate and wired fence, as up from the hold and then out onto the dockside emerged what was clearly Les's coffin.[49]

There! See? The spectators jostled each other, stood on tippy-toes to get a better look at the huge, ornate casket draped in its violet pall, covered in many wreaths and with such a sombre air about it that many people began to weep at its very sight. It seemed simply unbelievable that inside that box could lie the same Les Darcy so many of them knew personally, and nearly all had seen in the ring, or at least smiling back at them from the front and back pages of the newspapers. The Les they knew was so happy, so exuberant, so active, so everywhere at once, whether it was all around the ring or somewhere between Maitland and Melbourne and Memphis. And yet that sepulchre by the seaside was so still, so tragic, so damn *final* that the inherent human hope that all people have when they hear of a terrible death — that there must be some mistake, that there will be some kind of stunning follow-up news, and the person really is alive after all — itself died on the spot. A kind of collective moan went up from the crowd at hope's last gasp.

And there was Winnie, standing by the coffin, as the O'Sullivans — shocked to their core by how wan, thin and exhausted their girl appeared — tried to persuade her to return home to Paddington with them. But Winnie refused, insisting that her place was with Les, and she now formed up with the rest of the cortege as it made ready to leave the dockside and head for Wood Coffill & Co.'s funeral parlour on George Street.

As a band played a funeral march and the children from the local convent school at Millers Point recited the rosary and sang hymns, Les's coffin moved slowly out onto the streets of Sydney, and the mob parted like the Red Sea to make way for Moses. Many people were now sobbing openly, and yet not all ...

One little girl, Ruby, was in a state of confusion mixed with dreadful sorrow more than anything else.[50] That morning her mother had given her a handful of white feathers with the strict instruction that when Darcy's coffin passed her, she was to throw them on it. She was to do this in honour of her brother, who had so nobly died on the shores of Gallipoli. Her brother had done his duty, her mother said, but Darcy had not. He was a deserter and deserved to be treated this way.

And yet somehow, now that the moment was upon her, Ruby just couldn't do it. It wouldn't have been right. She kept her hands firmly in her pockets and threw the feathers away later, before returning home.

By that afternoon, Les's body was on full view in the open coffin, through the solid plate-glass windows at the undertaker's premises on George Street, as tens of thousands of Sydneysiders filed past — the women crying, the men trying not to. Beneath an enormous crucifix, with lighted candles all around throwing out an ethereal and flickering light, Les lay there, dressed in his Sunday best, eyes closed but looking content and at peace. Somehow death had shaved away the years, too, for Les seemed more boyish than ever, with not a single scar apparent, and it seemed impossible to imagine that in life he really had been nothing less than the middleweight champion of the world.

On and on the people came, in their droves, into the night. The pressure of the crowd against the plate-glass windows became so great at one point that with a dreadful scream of agony, they cracked and then collapsed. There were even more people there the next morning, and the desperate rush to see the great Darcy was so intense that traffic along

George Street was blocked and nearby businesses had to close down.

An extraordinarily poignant and yet still very powerful thing had happened as the body of Les Darcy had made its slow journey homewards. For the tragic circumstances of his death had not only neutralised most of the bitterness that had swirled about him in the last year of his life, but the once popular hero to beat them all was now being feted in death in the manner of a martyr — a secular saint of extraordinary courage who'd been brought low by evil forces. Those who had been on the attack dwindled and diminished, fell back and faltered, as the true Darcy loyalists swept all before them.

And there was something else in the air, too . . . something that the great Australian writer D'Arcy Niland would later put his finger on in most evocative tones. 'I don't think all those hundreds of thousands of people, millions really, were mourning for Les alone,' he wrote. 'Somewhere in the air was a vast silent lament for all the dead and ruined boys, the generation that had gone away laughing and singing and just vanished into thin air. In some mysterious way he was one of them, not a soldier but a battler, someone who did his best, came a cropper and didn't whinge about it. There's something profoundly perverse if you like, in the Australian psyche that feels most love for a good loser.'[51]

Whatever it was, it was as powerful as it was widespread. Two days later a Requiem Mass for Les was held at St Joseph's, Woollahra — the very church where he and Winnie had hoped to marry — and the streets all around were filled with wailing, groaning people. From the church, the cortege

— led by 200 boxers, of whom Dave Smith, Harold Hardwick and Jimmy Clabby were in the front row — was followed by huge crowds along the streets of Sydney to Central Station. The mourners behind the cortege were so dense that one eyewitness said, 'You could have walked on their heads like a sheepdog over a mob of woollies.' Flanking them down Oxford Street as they proceeded, the people stood twenty deep just to see the body go by, and the rooftops themselves were lined with the people of Sydney, silent sentinels against the sky, witnessing first-hand a funeral that would be talked about for generations to come. It was estimated that a quarter of a million people lined the route of the funeral procession.

And yet for this man, there would be more mourning still as, from Central Station, the body went by train to Maitland, where, after another Requiem Mass, Les would be taken home to his family. His coffin arrived at Maitland Railway Station on a bitterly cold Thursday night and, after being placed in a horse-drawn hearse — with the horses so cold they nearly shook off the harness[52] — it was driven straight to Father Coady's St Joseph's Church, where yet more people lined up to see it that night, and all day Friday, until a Requiem Mass was held on the Saturday morning.[53] At that point Les was taken, at last, into his mother's keeping at home at Lesleigh, where the body was to remain until the final funeral the following day.

From 11 o'clock on Saturday morning until 2 o'clock Saturday afternoon, Les remained in his glass-topped coffin in the high-ceilinged living room — with the roaring blaze in the fireplace never somehow removing the chill in the air — and a constant stream of people in black with their heads bowed came to view Australia's fallen son. Via the side door, at the rate of about fifty a minute,[54] they entered into the oppressive silence that surrounded Les's coffin, paused just long enough to soak up the sorrow of the scene and pay their respects, embraced Margaret Darcy and other members of the family, before heading out the front door.

And so to the funeral proper. Sunday morning dawned bright and clear, a perfect winter's morning, and the tiny country town soon found itself under a siege of sympathy. For they came from all corners ... in motorcars, on bicycles, in horse-drawn carriages and special trains from Sydney, Newcastle and the surrounding coalfields which were groaning with grievers. Many assembled at the Darcy household in East Maitland, or as near as they could get, while the majority lined both sides of the route between there and the cemetery, some four miles away, with every tree and telegraph pole along the way bearing mourners with bird's-eye views. Three cinematographic crews were there to record proceedings, one of which had come all the way from America.

Setting off at 3 pm, as the shadows of the wintry day were just beginning to lengthen, the cortege, with a procession two miles long behind it, was led by mounted police, followed by both the Maitland Federal Band and Singleton Band playing the funeral march.[55] The same boxers who had in Sydney walked at the head of the cortege were now joined by such locals as Billy McNabb, one of Les's first opponents, and also good ol' Fritz Holland, who had been touring with a vaudeville troupe somewhere in the vastness of Australia when he'd heard the terrible news of Les's death. Fritz had immediately dropped everything — no doubt including his opponent of the moment — and organised himself to be at Maitland for the last count to beat all last counts . . .

And a shocked Snowy Baker was there, too, a brave move considering how extreme people's emotions were running on the day and how high on the list of blame Baker was considered to be by many in that seething crowd.

Indeed, it was for good reason that at the cemetery Gentleman Dave Smith quietly took Snowy aside and strongly advised him against proceeding to the graveside. The feelings against Snowy were so ugly, he said, that some of the hotheads in the crowd were threatening to dig a grave right on the spot and bury Snowy alive, as his just desserts for what he had done to Les. Thinking that in this case discretion was likely the better part of valour, Snowy decided to withdraw and was soon on the road back to Sydney.[56]

A moment now, as the coffin-bearers — including the weeping Mick Hawkins at front on the right — steadied their cargo above the yawning cavity of mother earth. To the side, faint with misery, Winnie stood weeping, supported by the O'Sullivan clan. Up the front, with eight other priests, Father Joseph Coady was trying desperately not to join the two of them by releasing the agony in his heart and howling like a newborn child touched by a scalding iron.[57] The priest managed, just, to hold in his grief, but was infinitely glad that he had declined to speak at the graveside, knowing that his best hope of controlling his feelings was to maintain silence. Instead, the honour went to his colleague from West Maitland the Very Reverend Father F. O'Gorman. That good man now cleared his throat and began to speak to those of the throng who could hear him.

'It is the first time I have ever spoken in a cemetery,' he uttered in his grave, stentorian tones, which rolled over the heads of the milling mourners, 'and it will probably be the last. If I were to ask this vast multitude, and my voice could reach all, the question "Are you glad the remains of Les Darcy have been brought home to the land of his birth, to be clasped in her breast?" every hand, I feel sure, would go up in affirmation. So far as I am concerned, one of the proudest and pleasantest recollections of my life, will be the fact that I had a share in such a work. We Catholics are proud of Les Darcy, and never have we been prouder of him than today, for we are able to give to his calumniators the lie by virtue of this great demonstration by the public of this district. Before the grave closes over him, in his name, we can forgive his enemies, and though we may have cause of resentment, may we never refer to it again ...

'Had he gone on and reached the success he was striving after, he might never have realised what we knew him to be. All that is left to say is *Requiem aeternum*, to one of the noblest sons Australia has ever produced ...'[58]

And so it went.

They put the coffin into the vault, and that was the end.

Amen. Fare thee well, Les. You were a great Australian ...

EPILOGUE

It would take a Shakespeare to do justice to the poignant tragedy of Darcy's life, to an assessment of his outstanding qualities, to the one great conflict he could not handle, that of the clash of two worthy ideals, — love of parents and love of his native land . . . Here was a modern Hamlet, bringing to an untimely end the bloom of a brilliant career because one honest motive grappled with another. Here is depicted tragedy, success and failure, enveloping an extraordinary character, with a background typical of that of Australian pioneering itself, struggling, fighting heavy odds, assuming undue responsibilities, and withal, maintaining an ubiquitous and infectious optimism and cheerfulness. Les Darcy grew out, not in . . .

WRITER T.J. MORAN, QUOTED IN THE *NEWCASTLE MORNING HERALD AND MINERS ADVOCATE*, ON 13 DECEMBER 1944, IN WHAT THE AUTHOR CONSIDERS IS THE BEST AND MOST CONCISE SUMMATION OF LES DARCY'S LIFE. MORAN KNEW DARCY WELL PERSONALLY

For as long as four years after Les Darcy's death it was still possible to view his body in his glass-topped coffin in its vault, at which point the deterioration was marked enough that the vault was closed permanently.

These days East Maitland cemetery stands in a distinctly unprepossessing industrial area, with a railway line marking its southwestern edge and a busy road on another. Nevertheless, while there is a rather depressing air of neglect and desiccation that hangs over it all, there is no problem in spotting Les's grave. It is the one that stands out huge from the others, almost as if the people who placed it there wanted to send a message to future generations about what this bloke had meant to them in their time.

The legend of Darcy remained strong throughout Australia right up until the mid-1960s, before slumbering for a while and then reviving somewhat in the mid-1990s, at the centenary of his birth. Les's place in the boxing firmament of major stars was at least secured in October of 1998 when his name was inducted into the World Boxing Hall of Fame in Los Angeles, taking its place alongside the likes of Muhammad Ali, Joe Frazier, Joe Louis and Sugar Ray Robinson, as well as such Australian greats as Johnny Famechon and Lionel Rose.

Margaret Darcy never quite got over the death of Les. It was a grief that was compounded over the course of the following ten years as first her next son, Frosty, died in 1919, after contracting the Spanish flu, followed by two more of her children from illness. And yet, the fact that the legend of Les lived on meant that in many ways he did too for her, and the youngest of her children — Joe, who lived until 1989 — recorded that when visitors, often authors and journalists, would come to his mother to discuss the actions of Les, she had a stock answer: 'Whether Les was right or wrong, only time will tell ...'[1]

Margaret herself died in 1929, aged fifty-seven, and she, with most of the rest of the Darcy family, is buried in the same vault wherein lies Les. Ned Darcy lived until the age of seventy-seven and died in 1936.

Father Joe Coady wore a photo of Les in a medallion on his priestly garb for the rest of his long life, and was also a veritable keeper of the flame as far as Les went.[2] He, too, had a well-considered line with which he responded to questions about his favourite communicant: 'Les Darcy was born to greatness. Had he not chosen to make boxing his career, there is no doubt he would have become a great statesman or prominent figure whichever field he chose.'[3] Father Coady died in 1959, at which point he was the parish priest at Merewether near Newcastle.

Maurice O'Sullivan went on to take over as the licensee of the Lord Dudley Hotel before embarking on a very successful career in the NSW State Parliament, rising to the position of long-time Minister for Health and Transport in a series of Labor governments. He died in 1972.

Tim O'Sullivan stayed on in America for several years after Darcy's death, building a successful career there as a racehorse trainer, before going to England where he accomplished the same thing. When World War II broke out, he transferred his operations to Ireland for the duration, and then went back to England and France after the war was over. He returned to

Australia in 1958, after forty-two years away, and continued to train horses, mostly around Warwick Farm in Sydney's southwest. In the mid-1960s, just a couple of years before he died, Tim O'Sullivan was tracked down by a postmaster from Newcastle, Bob Power, who wanted to talk to him extensively about his time with Les Darcy. O'Sullivan, after decades of batting off such requests, agreed, and in the end trusted Power so much, he bequeathed him an extremely precious scrapbook, containing many newspaper cuttings from his time with Darcy in America — a document that now resides in the archives of Newcastle University Library.

And what about Tommy Burns, who had so famously fought and lost against Jack Johnson at the Sydney Stadium in 1908? Tommy's end is worth telling, if for no other reason than it presents no greater contrast than that of Les's.

Though he continued to fight until 1920, Tommy died destitute in Vancouver, British Columbia, in 1958 aged seventy-three, and just four people attended his funeral, during which he was placed in a pauper's grave with no stone to tell where he lay.

Jack Johnson had a chequered career after beating Tommy Burns. Appalled at the result, many powerbrokers in American boxing began the search to find a 'great white hope' to beat Johnson. In desperation pure, the former world heavyweight champion Jim Jeffries was induced to come out of his six-year retirement, and before his bout against Johnson in Reno, Nevada, on 4 July 1910, no less than the *New York*

Times editorialised: 'If the black man wins, thousands and thousands of his ignorant brothers will misinterpret victory as justifying claims to much more than mere physical equality with their white neighbours.'[4]

As it happened, despite the all-white crowd chanting 'Kill the nigger!' throughout, the black man *did* win. What scandalised much of America even more was that Johnson went on to marry and keep company with a succession of *white* women!

Even when a white cowboy, Jess Willard, finally beat Johnson in April 1915, still white America did not forgive him. In 1920, Johnson was charged with having sent his white girlfriend a train ticket to travel from Pittsburgh to Chicago, and was subsequently convicted of 'transporting women across state lines for immoral purposes' — a law designed to stop prostitution. In a gross miscarriage of justice he served a year in Leavenworth Federal penitentiary. Once released, Johnson kept fighting until 1928, when he opened a nightclub. He died in a car crash in 1946 at the age of sixty-eight, but his legend lived on. In his own career, Muhammad Ali constantly referred to Jack Johnson as one of his inspirations.

Eddie McGoorty, perhaps Les's most famous opponent, joined the American Army shortly after the United States entered the war in 1917, and served out his time in the relative safety of being a physical instructor — interspersed with fighting various heavyweight bouts against members of other armed forces. After the war he kept fighting until he retired in 1922, and went on to open a gym in Chicago. He developed tuberculosis and died at the relatively young age of forty. In all the boxing literature of the time, no one appears to have had a single bad word to say about him. (And in terms of sporting heroes taking the relatively easy option of becoming physical instructors for their national army when war breaks out, it is worth noting that it was precisely the option taken, with almost no controversy, by the man who was Australia's greatest sporting hero when World War II began — Donald Bradman.)

As to Young Griffo, the brilliant Australian boxing champion who preceded Les Darcy travelling to America by a couple of decades, he continued his slow descent from the time he met Les, and finished his life as a perhaps punch-drunk panhandler in New York's Times Square, and was a well-known local character sitting on the steps of the Rialto Theatre, with his cap out before him. It is said, though not confirmed, that when Griffo died in 1927, the promoter Tex Rickard saluted what he had once been by paying for his funeral.

Harold Hardwick, who fired off the punch that broke Les's teeth, went on to live a full and happy life, reaching professional heights as the Deputy Director of Physical Education for the NSW Education Department.[5] After hours, he was a very active and successful swimming coach — and among his junior charges at Bankstown swimming pool in 1952 was the eight-year-old Ilsa Konrads, who would go on to smash many world records and win a silver medal at the Rome Olympics in 1960.

★

The dandy with a nose for boxing talent, Jack Kearns, overcame his disappointment at not managing Les Darcy and went on to manage an American pugilist of some note, a fellow by the name of Jack Dempsey ... who reigned as world heavyweight champion from 1919 to 1926. One of Dempsey's successful defences of his title was against none other than Georges Carpentier, who, after being awarded two of the highest French military honours, the Croix de Guerre and the Médaille Militaire for his derring-do with the French Airforce in the war, had resumed his boxing career.[6]

The Carpentier versus Dempsey fight in 1921 is credited with being boxing's first million-dollar gate, which was some recompense to the Frenchman, given that he was brutally knocked out by Dempsey in the second minute of the fourth round. Carpentier never fought for the title again, and shortly afterwards retired. Nevertheless, a fruitful life followed, which included great success as an actor and then as an upscale bar owner in Paris. Born the year before Les Darcy, in 1894, he lived nearly sixty years longer than his Australian counterpart, dying in 1975. His grave is in Vaires-sur-Marne, France.

In 1917, Billy Hughes once again tried to introduce conscription and once again failed. Alas, the loss of lives and limbs of Australian soldiers who were in the war of their own free will continued on a massive scale, and from July to November of 1917, almost 40,000 were killed or injured — the heaviest casualty rate of any Allied country in the war.

Hughes's most famous moment as Prime Minister, or at least the most recounted, came during the post-World War I peace conference at the Palace of Versailles, in an exchange with the seemingly all-powerful President Wilson of the United States of America. At issue was who would now have control of the formerly German colony in New Guinea. The American favoured Japan, which had fought on the side of the Allies in the war, while Hughes was equally insistent that it should be Australia. When a frustrated Wilson sought to cut Hughes down by noting that 'After all, you speak for only five million people', Hughes dryly replied: 'I speak for 60,000 dead. For how many do you speak?'[7]

Hughes won that argument and remained Prime Minister until 9 February 1923, and was a member of parliament until he died on 28 October 1952. He is still the longest serving parliamentarian in Australian history, a longevity that stands in marked contrast to the political career of Charles S. Whitman, whose American presidential ambitions were thwarted when he lost the New York governorship in 1918, and never recovered.

In February 1918, the Sydney Stadium closed its doors for want of both fighters and crowds. Snowy Baker then turned his attention to acting in and producing silent films, with his debut as an actor coming in *The Enemy Within*, in which he portrayed a dashing secret agent who has returned from World War I and is now going after a spy ring. While Baker's co-star in the film — none other than Lily Molloy, who played the part of his girlfriend — was panned for her performance, Baker himself received such critical acclaim he was able to launch himself into Hollywood. There, he also worked as a stuntman and instructor in various skills — and in the course of his long career he was credited with teaching Elizabeth Taylor how to ride a horse and Rudolph Valentino how to kiss. Baker died in 1953, outliving H.D. McIntosh by eleven years.

And Winnie, sitting there on the 24th of May, 1967 in the front pew at St Francis' Church, Paddington, for the Les Darcy Fifty-Year Memorial Service, opening and closing the tiny gold locket she has in her pocket? She has had a tough, but full life in the fifty years to the day since Les died. She took a long time to recover from the death of her great love, but in 1921, at the age of twenty-five, she married a racehorse trainer by the name of Edmond Hannan, with whom she had two sons in quick succession. Alas, only six years after the wedding, her husband also died after a sudden illness, leaving her with two infants to bring up on her own. This she did successfully, with the help of the wider O'Sullivan clan — most particularly including her brother Maurice. She was never to remarry. From time to time people would ask her about Les Darcy and, though she was always polite, it was not a subject that she warmed to easily.

All of that was so long ago. Another time ... Another place ...

Still, she had that locket with her until the day she died, in 1974, at the age of eighty ...

Vale, Winnie.

ENDNOTES

Chapter 1 — Way Back When

1   In fact, it was not Tennyson who said this, but Henry
    Wadsworth Longfellow in his poem, 'A Psalm of Life':
    Lives of great men all remind us
    We can make our lives sublime,
    And, departing, leave behind us
    Footprints on the sands of time;

2   www.historyplace.com/worldhistory/famine/ruin.htm

3   www.historyplace.com/worldhistory/famine/ruin.htm

4   Quoted in Sir Charles Trevelyan, 'The Irish Crisis, Being a
    Narrative of the Measures for the Relief of the Distress
    Caused by the Great Irish Famine of 1846–7', London 1880,
    reproduced from the *Edinburgh Review* 175, Jan. 1848.

5   Sir Charles Trevelyan, 'The Irish Crisis'.

6   Ruth Park and Rafe Champion, *Home Before Dark*, Viking,
    Ringwood, Vic. 1995, p. 17.

7   *Newcastle Morning Herald and Miners Advocate*, 16 Dec. 1947.

8   *Newcastle Morning Herald and Miners Advocate*, 16 Dec. 1947.

9   Park and Champion, *Home Before Dark*, p. 19.

10 Raymond Swanwick, *Les Darcy: Australia's Golden Boy of
    Boxing*, Ure Smith, Sydney, 1965, p. 10.

11 Ken Burns (dir.) *Unforgivable Blackness: The Rise and Fall of
    Jack Johnson*, documentary, Florentine Films and WETA
    Washington, DC, 2005.

12 Joe Darcy, 'My Brother Les', *Hunter Manning Magazine*, 20 Jun. 1977.

13 *Maitland Daily Mercury*, quoted in Bob Power, *The Les Darcy American Venture* self-published, New Lambton, NSW, 1994, p. 7.

14 *Newcastle Morning Herald and Miners Advocate*, 16 Dec. 1947. The paper ran a series of articles marking thirty years since Les Darcy's death.

15 *Newcastle Morning Herald and Miners Advocate*, 5 Nov. 1912.

16 Park and Champion, *Home Before Dark*, p. 60.

17 John Molony, *The Penguin History of Australia*, Penguin, Ringwood, Vic., 1988, p. 206.

18 For the record, this was his fighting name only. His real name was Arthur Patton, which is why it took me so long to pick up a trace of him at the Australian War Memorial. For the simplicity of the account, I have left it as Regio Delaney throughout.

19 *Newcastle Morning Herald and Miners Advocate*, 18 Dec. 1947

20 *Newcastle Morning Herald and Miners Advocate*, 18 Dec. 1947.

21 *Newcastle Morning Herald and Miners Advocate*, 20 Dec. 1947.

22 Park and Champion, *Home Before Dark*, p. 71.

23 *Maitland Daily Mercury*, quoted in Bob Power, *The Les Darcy American Venture*, p. 8.

24 Bob Power, *The Les Darcy American Venture*, p. 11.

25 *Newcastle Morning Herald and Miners Advocate*, 20 May 1967.

Chapter 2 — Let Slip the Dogs of War

1 www.bbc.co.uk/dna/h2g2/A11873900.

2 *Sydney Morning Herald*, 30 Jun. 1914.

3 *Daily Telegraph*, Sydney, 29 Jun. 1914.

4 *Catholic Weekly*, 14 Aug. 1958. The accounts from a series of articles that ran in the paper at this time called the 'Priest and the Boxer' are particularly interesting, as they are based on a rare interview with Father Coady himself.

5   Raymond Swanwick, *Les Darcy: Australia's Golden Boy of Boxing*, p. 67. For a report of the fight see also *Sydney Morning Herald*, 20 Jul. 1914.

6   Park and Champion, *Home Before Dark*, p. 89.

7   *Argus*, 1 Aug. 1914.

8   *Sydney Morning Herald*, 6 Aug. 1914.

9   Peter Dennis, Jeffrey Grey, Ewan Morris, Robin Prior and John Connor, *The Oxford Companion to Australian Military History*, Oxford University Press, Melbourne, 1995, p. 237

10 Park and Champion, *Home Before Dark*, p. 105.

11 Park and Champion, *Home Before Dark*, p. 96.

12 Bob Power, *The Les Darcy American Venture*, p. 33.

13 Georges Carpentier avec Jacques Marchand, *Mes 80 Rounds*, ed. Olivier Orban, 1975, p. 112.

14 *Catholic Weekly*, 14 Aug. 1958.

15 Raymond Swanwick, *Les Darcy, Australia's Golden Boy of Boxing*, p. 80.

Chapter 3 — Heroes

1   Park and Champion, *Home Before Dark*, p. 96.

2   *Newcastle Morning Herald and Miners Advocate*, 26 Dec. 1947.

3   *Newcastle Morning Herald and Miners Advocate*, 19 Dec. 1947.

4   P.V. Vernon, OBE, ED (ed.), *The Royal New South Wales Lancers 1885–1985: Incorporating a Narrative of the 1st Light Horse Regiment, AIF, 1914–1919*, Royal New South Wales Lancers Centenary Committee, Parramatta, NSW, 1986, p. 162.

5   P.V. Vernon, OBE, ED (ed.), *The Royal New South Wales Lancers 1885–1985*, p. 93.

6   *Newcastle Morning Herald and Miners Advocate*, 26 Dec. 1947.

7   *Newcastle Morning Herald and Miners Advocate*, 26 Dec. 1947.

8   *Sporting Life*, Jun. 1953.

9   *Sunday Times*, Sydney, 1 Aug. 1915.

10 *Sunday Times*, Sydney, 1 Aug. 1915.

11 *Sunday Times*, Sydney, 1 Aug. 1915.

12 *Newcastle Morning Herald and Miners Advocate*, 26 Dec. 1947.

13 Raymond Swanwick, *Les Darcy: Australia's Golden Boy of Boxing*, p. 128.

14 Park and Champion, *Home Before Dark*, p. 161.

15 Park and Champion, *Home Before Dark*, p. 162.

16 As quoted in Bob Power, *The Les Darcy American Venture*, p. 27.

17 Paige Reynolds, *Modernist Martyrdom: The Funerals of Terence MacSwiney*, Vol. 9, No. 4, Johns Hopkins University, Nov. 2002, pp. 535–59.

18 Park and Champion, *Home Before Dark*, p. 165.

19 As quoted in John Hamilton, *Goodbye Cobber, God Bless You*, Pan Macmillan, Sydney, 2004, p. 243.

20 P.V. Vernon, OBE, ED (ed.), *The Royal New South Wales Lancers 1885–1985*, p. 94.

21 Tolga Ornek (dir.), *Gallipoli*, documentary, Epik Film, Turkey, 2005.

22 John Hamilton, *Goodbye Cobber, God Bless You*, p. 309.

23 I was unable to locate the actual cables, and the two cables here are only representative of the generic form of such cables at the time.

24 *Daily Telegraph*, Sydney, 1 Sep. 1947.

25 Bob Power, *The Les Darcy American Venture,* p. 7.

26 *Newcastle Morning Herald and Miners Advocate*, 30 Dec. 1947.

27 Interview with Winnie's son, Fr Kevin Hannan, 20 Dec. 2006.

28 Park and Champion, *Home Before Dark*, p. 201.

29 Park and Champion, *Home Before Dark*, p. 201.

Chapter 4 — A Cold Win Blows

1 Bob Power, *The Les Darcy American Venture*, p. 35.

2 *Sporting Life*, Jun. 1953. Les Darcy also referred to this in the piece he penned for *New York World*, entitled 'Les Darcy Insists He Is Not A Shirker', on 24 Dec., 1916: 'Hugh McIntosh was arranging to take me out of the country [early in 1916]. When he thought others were going to do it, he set about preventing my going away.'

3　This account was provided by Darcy's great friend Mick Tobin to author Bob Power in the late 1960s, when Bob Power was researching his book *The Les Darcy American Venture*.

4　Quoted in Bob Power, *The Les Darcy American Venture*, p. 36.

5　Murray G. Phillips and Katharine Moore, 'The Champion Boxer Les Darcy: A Victim of Class Conflict and Sectarian Bitterness in Australia During the First World War', *International Journal of the History of Sport*, Vol. 11, No. 1, Apr. 1994, 102–114 at p. 104.

6　Bob Power, *The Les Darcy American Venture*, p. 37.

7　Based on the recollections of Mick Hawkins in *Sporting Life*, Jun. 1953.

8　Joe Darcy, 'My Brother Les', *Hunter Manning Magazine*, 20 Jun. 1977.

9　www.irishfreedom.net/Articles/A%20century%20of% 20lost%20opportunities.htm

10　Donald Horne, *In Search of Billy Hughes*, Macmillan, Melbourne, 1979, p. 65.

11　Joe Darcy, 'My Brother Les', *Hunter Manning Magazine*, 20 Jun. 1977.

12　*Newcastle Morning Herald and Miners Advocate*, 30 Dec. 1947.

13　*Sports Novels*, Jul. 1947.

14　*Sports Novels*, Jul. 1947.

15　The fighter in question was Harry Greb. www.cyberboxingzone.com/boxing/gibbons-m.html

16　*Newcastle Morning Herald and Miners Advocate*, 13 Dec. 1944.

17　Margaret Young and Bill Gammage (eds), *Hail and Farewell: Letters From Two Brothers Killed in France in 1916, Alec and Goldy Raws*, Kangaroo Press, Kenthurst, NSW, 1995, pp. 147–148.

18　Young and Gammage, *Hail and Farewell*, p. 145.

19　Donald Horne, *In Search of Billy Hughes*, p. 70.

20　Account of this death held by the Australian War Memorial www.awm.gov.au/cms_images/1DRL428/00027/1DRL428-00027-2100802.pdf

21 Garrie Hutchinson, *Pilgrimage: A Traveller's Guide to Australia's Battlefields*, Black Inc., Melbourne, 2006, p. 119.

22 Donald Horne, *In Search of Billy Hughes*, p. 71.

23 *Daily Standard*, Brisbane, 15 Aug. 1916.

24 *Melbourne Herald*, 24 Aug. 1916.

25 Park and Champion, *Home Before Dark*, p. 214.

26 Bob Power, *The Les Darcy American Venture*, p. 40.

27 Bob Power, *The Les Darcy American Venture*, p. 39.

28 In a letter to Father Coady on 12 Apr. 1917, Les wrote, 'We got talking about conscription coming on, and he expressed a desire to get out of the country before the vote was taken, and of course I was just as anxious to get away', quoted in Bob Power, *The Les Darcy American Venture*, p. 39.

29 Letter from Tim O'Sullivan to W.F. Corbett, published in the *Referee*, 14 Jul. 1917.

30 L.F. Fitzhardinge, *The Little Digger, 1914–1952: William Morris Hughes, A Political Biography*, Vol. 2, Angus & Robertson Publishers, Sydney, 1979, p. 182.

31 Bob Power, *The Les Darcy American Venture*, p. 41.

32 www.members.optushome.com.au/spainter/Catholics.html

33 www.members.optushome.com.au/spainter/Catholics.html

34 Donald Horne, *In Search of Billy Hughes*, p. 76.

35 Donald Horne, *In Search of Billy Hughes*, p. 79.

36 *Sydney Morning Herald*, 19 Sep. 1916.

37 'The Vital Argument', in *Australian Worker*, 7 Sep. 1916. p. 17. The article was probably written by Henry Ernest Boote, who was the editor of the publication at the time.

38 *Sydney Morning Herald*, 19 Sep. 1916.

39 *Brisbane Worker*, 12 Oct. 1916.

40 *Rewind*, ABC TV, episode broadcast 24 Oct. 2004.

41 *Newcastle Morning Herald and Miners Advocate*, 16 Dec. 1947.

42 *Sporting Life*, Jun. 1953.

43 Bob Power, *The Les Darcy American Venture*, p. 47.

44 *Newcastle Herald*, 17 Oct. 1984.

45 *Catholic Weekly*, 14 Aug. 1958. Also in the car with Les and Fr Coady was Les's friend Mick Tobin, who later talked about it expansively to the author Bob Power.

46 Bob Power, *The Les Darcy American Venture*, p. 50.

47 Bob Power, *The Les Darcy American Venture*, p. 53.

48 Raymond Swanwick, *Les Darcy: Australia's Golden Boy of Boxing*, p. 192.

49 *Daily Mirror*, Sydney, 31 Oct. 1916.

50 *Daily Mirror*, Sydney, 31 Oct. 1916.

51 Peter Fenton, *Les Darcy: The Legend of a Fighting Man*, Ironbark Press, Chippendale, NSW, 1994.

Chapter 5 — America

1 *New York Evening Journal*, 23 Dec., as reprinted in *Maitland Daily Mercury*, 3 Feb. 1917.

2 *New York World*, 24 Dec. 1916.

3 Raymond Swanwick, *Les Darcy: Australia's Golden Boy of Boxing*, p. 201.

4 From a Sydney paper possibly printed in early January 1917, but the markings on the clipping are not clear. It is contained in the scrapbook originally belonging to Tim O'Sullivan, now held in Newcastle University Archives.

5 Ruth Park, article about Les Darcy, in the *National Times*, 30 Dec. 1978.

6 Letter held by National Library of Australia. www.nla.gov.au/nla.pic-vn3050323

7 Letter held by National Library of Australia. www.nla.gov.au/nla.pic-vn3050323

8 Park and Champion, *Home Before Dark*, p. 260.

9 Owen Eric Newton, war dossier, http://naa12.naa.gov.au/scripts/Imagine.asp

10 Bob Power, *The Les Darcy American Venture*, p. 69.

11 *New York World*, 16 Jan. 1917.

12 *New York World*, 16 Feb. 1917.

13 *Catholic Weekly*, 7 Aug. 1958.

14 Park and Champion, *Home Before Dark*, p. 286.

15 *New York Times*, 3 Mar. 1917.

16 *Globe and Commercial Advertiser,* New York, 26 May 1917.

17 Which particular New York paper this is from is not clear in the scrapbook of articles that Tim O'Sullivan kept, but it is from a wire service story marked 'Albany N.Y. March 7'.

18 *Sporting Globe*, Melbourne, 13 Jan. 1954.

19 *Daily Telegraph*, Sydney, 12 May 1917, as quoted in Phillips and Moore, 'The Champion Boxer Les Darcy: A Victim of Class Conflict and Sectarian Bitterness in Australia During the First World War', *International Journal of the History of Sport*, p. 109.

20 Ruth Park, article about Les Darcy in *National Times*, 30 Dec. 1978.

21 *Cleveland Press*, 31 Mar. 1917.

22 John L. Heaton (ed.), *Cobb of 'the World'* (1924), reprinted in Henry Steele Commager and Allan Nevins, *The Heritage of America* (1939); Robert H. Ferrell, *Woodrow Wilson and World War I* (1986); David M. Kennedy, *Over Here: The First World War and American Society* (1980). See also www.eyewitnesstohistory.com/wilsonwar.htm

23 John L. Heaton (ed.), *Cobb of 'the World'*.

24 Tim O'Sullivan scrapbook, Newcastle University Archives.

25 *New York Times*, 14 Apr. 1917.

26 Letter from Les Darcy to Maurice O'Sullivan, dated 15 Apr. 1917, held at the Australian Gallery of Sport and Olympic Museum, Melbourne.

27 Tim O'Sullivan scrapbook, Newcastle University Archives.

28 Park and Champion, *Home Before Dark*, p. 314.

29 *New York Times*, 21 Apr. 1917.

30 This detail is mentioned in a letter from Les Darcy to his friend Mick Stapleton in Australia, written on 21 Apr. 1917, from the Peabody Hotel in Memphis, and quoted in Bob Power, *The Les Darcy American Venture*, p. 99.

31 *New York World*, 25 Apr. 1917.

32 *New York Tribune*, 24 Apr. 1917.

33 Park and Champion, *Home Before Dark*, p. 286.

34 Park and Champion, *Home Before Dark*, p. 320.

35 Ruth Park, article in *National Times*, 6 Jan. 1979.

36 *Catholic Weekly*, 28 Aug. 1958.

37 *Catholic Weekly*, 28 Aug. 1958.

38 Park and Champion, *Home Before Dark*, p. 328.

39 *Australian Magazine*, 30 Sep. – 1 Oct. 1995.

40 Park and Champion, *Home Before Dark*, p. 330.

41 Ruth Park, article in *National Times*, 30 Dec. 1978.

42 *Referee*, 4 Jul. 1917.

43 Mick's own account of the moment of death was reported in the *Sporting Globe*, 13 Jan. 1954: 'His eyelids fluttered, closed, and he was gone. We all broke down and cried bitterly, even the doctors and nurses. They had all learned to love him, and admired his plucky, uncomplaining long fight against death.'

44 According to a copy of the Memphis death certificate.

45 Park and Champion, *Home Before Dark*, p. 334.

46 'The Little Things I Remember About My Brother', *Newcastle Sun*, 26 Feb. 1979.

47 *Newcastle Morning Herald and Miners Advocate*, 2 Jul. 1917.

48 Raymond Swanwick, *Les Darcy: Australia's Golden Boy of Boxing*, p.230.

49 A full report of the arrival of the *Sonoma*, and Les's casket was provided in the *Referee*, 4 Jul. 1917.

50 Park and Champion, *Home Before Dark*, p. 2.

51 Park and Champion, *Home Before Dark*, p. 353.

52 'He Drove Darcy's Hearse', *Maitland Daily Mercury*, 3 Mar. 1975, quoting the driver of the hearse, Stan Fairhall.

53 *Referee*, 4 Jul. 1917.

54 *Maitland Daily Mercury*, 2 Jul. 1917.

55 *Maitland Daily Mercury*, 2 Jul. 1917.

56 *Sydney Sportsman*, 17 Jul. 1917.

57 As acknowledged by Father Coady in a conversation with Bob Power in the 1950s.

58 *Newcastle Morning Herald and Miners Advocate*, 2 Jul. 1917.

Epilogue

1   Joe Darcy, 'My Brother Les', *Hunter Manning Magazine*, 20 Jun. 1977.

2   Joe Darcy, 'My Brother Les', *Hunter Manning Magazine*, 20 Jun. 1977

3   Joe Darcy, 'My Brother Les', *Hunter Manning Magazine*, 20 Jun. 1977

4   *New York Times*, 12 May 1910.

5   *Sporting Life*, Jun. 1953.

6   Georges Carpentier, *Mes 80 Rounds*, p. 222.

7   Peter Luck, *This Fabulous Century*, Landsdowne Press, Sydney, 1980.

SELECT BIBLIOGRAPHY

C.E.W. Bean, *The Story of Anzac,* Angus & Robertson, Sydney, 1924, Vol. 1.

Georges Carpentier avec Jacques Marchand, *Mes 80 Rounds*, ed. Olivier Orban, 1975.

Peter Corris, *Lords of the Ring: A Social History of Prize Fighting in Australia*, Cassell Australia, Melbourne, 1980

Peter Fenton, Les Darcy, *The Legend of the Fighting Man*, Ironbark Press, Chippendale, NSW, 1994

L.F. Fitzhardinge, *The Little Digger, 1914–1952: William Morris Hughes, A Political Biography*, Vol. 2, Angus & Robertson Publishers, Sydney, 1979

Greg Growden, *The Snowy Baker Story*, Random House Australia, Milsons Point, NSW, 2003

John Hamilton, *Goodbye Cobber, God Bless You*, Pan Macmillan, Sydney, 2004

Donald Horne, *In Search of Billy Hughes*, Macmillan, Melbourne, 1979

Garrie Hutchinson, *Pilgrimage: A Traveller's Guide to Australia's Battlefields*, Black Inc., Melbourne, 2006

Peter Luck, *This Fabulous Century*, Lansdowne Press, Sydney, 1980

Mason, K.J., *Experience of Nationhood: Australia and the World Since 1900*, McGraw Hill, Sydney, 1975

John Molony, *The Penguin History of Australia*, Penguin, Ringwood, Vic., 1988

Patrick O'Farrell, *The Irish in Australia: 1788 to the Present*, Sydney, UNSW Press, 2000

Ruth Park and Rafe Champion, *Home Before Dark*, Viking, Ringwood, Vic. 1995

Bob Power, *Fighters of the North*, self-published, New Lambton, NSW, 1976

Bob Power, *The Les Darcy American Venture*, self-published, New Lambton, NSW, 1994

James B. Roberts and Alexander G. Skutt, *The Boxing Register*, McBooks Press, 1999

Raymond Swanwick, *Les Darcy: Australia's Golden Boy of Boxing*, Ure Smith, Sydney, 1965

Sir Charles Trevelyan, 'The Irish Crisis, Being a Narrative of the Measures for the Relief of the Distress Caused by the Great Irish Famine of 1846–7', London, 1880

P.V. Vernon, OBE, ED (ed.), *The Royal New South Wales Lancers 1885–1985: Incorporating a Narrative of the 1st Light Horse Regiment, AIF, 1914–1919*, Royal New South Wales Lancers Centenary Committee, Parramatta, NSW, 1986

Brian Walsh and Cameron Archer, *Maitland on the Hunter*, C.B. Alexander Foundation, Paterson, NSW, 2000

Margaret Young and Bill Gammage (eds), *Hail and Farewell: Letters From Two Brothers Killed in France in 1916. Alec and Goldy Raws*, Kangaroo Press, Kenthurst, NSW, 1995

Peter Dennis, Jeffrey Grey, Ewan Morris, Robin Prior and John Connor, *The Oxford Companion to Australian Military History*, Oxford University Press, Melbourne, 1995

Academic Papers

There has been a fair measure of academic work done on Les Darcy over the years but, in my view, none finer, wider or deeper than that done by Murray G. Phillips and Katharine Moore, who were at the University of Canberra and the University of Alberta, respectively, when they did the work that I cite below.

Murray G. Phillips and Katharine Moore, 'The Champion Boxer
Les Darcy: A Victim of Class Conflict and Sectarian Bitterness
in Australia During the First World War', *International Journal
of the History of Sport*, Vol. 11, No. 1, Apr. 1994

Murray G. Phillips and Katharine Moore, 'From Adulation to
Persecution and Back in America 1916-1917', *Journal of Sport
History*, Vol. 23. No. 1, 1996

Paige Reynolds, *Modernist Martyrdom; the Funerals of Terence
MacSwiney*, Vol. 9, No. 4, Johns Hopkins University Press, Nov.
2002, pp. 535–59.

Peter FitzSimons is a journalist with the *Sydney Morning Herald* and *Sun-Herald*, a frequent contributor to the London *Daily Telegraph*, a breakfast radio broadcaster on 2UE954AM in Sydney, and has interviewed everyone from President George Bush Snr to Edmund Hillary to Diego Maradona. He is also a popular after-dinner speaker and the only Wallaby sent from the field against the All Blacks — unjustly, he swears. Peter is the author of seventeen other books — including biographies of Nancy Wake, Kim Beazley, Nene King, Nick Farr-Jones, Steve Waugh and John Eales — and was Australia's bestselling non-fiction writer in 2001, 2004 and 2006. His last military work was the number-one bestselling book *Tobruk*. He lives with his journalist wife, Lisa Wilkinson, and their three young children in Sydney.